ANIMAL MECHANICALS

Insects and Spiders

Tom Jackson

PowerKiDS
press

Published in 2017 by
The Rosen Publishing Group, Inc.
29 East 21st Street, New York, NY 10010

Cataloging-in-Publication Data

Names: Jackson, Tom.
Title: Insects and spiders / Tom Jackson.
Description: New York : PowerKids Press, 2017. | Series: Animal mechanicals | Includes index.
Identifiers: ISBN 9781508150305 (pbk.) | ISBN 9781508150244 (library bound) | ISBN 9781508150121 (6 pack)
Subjects: LCSH: Insects--Juvenile literature. | Spiders--Juvenile literature.
Classification: LCC QL467.2 J32 2017 | DDC 595.7--dc23

For Brown Bear Books Ltd:
Editorial Director: Lindsey Lowe
Editor: Tom Jackson
Children's Publisher: Anne O'Daly
Design Manager: Keith Davis
Designer: Lynne Lennon
Picture Manager: Sophie Mortimer

Picture Credits
T=Top, C=Center, B=Bottom, L=Left, R=Right
Front Cover: 1st swatch, ©Shutterstock/Marco Uliana; 2nd swatch, ©Shutterstock/Protasov AN; 3rd swatch, ©Shutterstock/Tischenko Irina; butterfly, ©Shutterstock/Butterfly Hunter; dung beetle, ©Shutterstock/Four Oaks; tarantula, ©Shutterstock/Aleksey Stemmer; stick insect, ©Shutterstock/Soultkd; bee, ©Shutterstock/irin-k / Shutterstock; chrysalis illustration, ©Shutterstock/Capreola; push pins, ©Shutterstock/Picsfive; lined paper, ©Shutterstock/Yuttasak Jannarong. **Inside:** 1, ©Shutterstock/In Love Pal; 4cl, ©Shutterstock/Imfoto; 4bl, ©Shutterstock/Sebastian Janicki; 5, ©Shutterstock/Bildagentur Zooner GmbH; 6, ©Shutterstock/Sergio Sallovitz; 7, ©Shutterstock/Dr. Morey Read; 8/9, ©Shutterstock/Aleksey Stemmer; 9tr, ©Shutterstock/Kritskaya; 9cr, ©Shutterstock/Asamin Images; 10/11, ©Shutterstock/Radka Palenikova; 11t, ©Thinkstock/Clandy Images/iStock; 11c, ©Shutterstock/Steven Ellingson; 12/13, ©Shutterstock/Wacpan; 13, ©Shutterstock/Reptiles4all; 14/15, ©Shutterstock/Cosmin Manci; 15, ©Shutterstock/Quang Ho; 16/17, ©Shutterstock/Four Oaks; 17c, ©Shutterstock/Tomatito; 17cr, ©Shutterstock/Henrik Larsson; 18, ©Shutterstock/Erik Karlts; 19l, ©Shutterstock/Natalya Aksenova; 19r, ©Shutterstock/Bildagentur Zooner GmbH; 20, ©Shutterstock/In Love Pal; 21cl, ©Shutterstock/Serg64; 21cr, ©Shutterstock/Light Poet; 21br, ©Shutterstock/Roberaten; 22, ©Shutterstock/Little Sam; 22tc, ©Shutterstock/Blues Note; 22tr, ©Shutterstock/Paul Rommer; 23c, ©Shutterstock/Alexey Stlap; 24/25, ©Shutterstock/Lakeview Images; 25, ©Shutterstock/Sam D Cruz; 26, ©Shutterstock/Cathy Keifer; 26/27, ©Shutterstock/Sarl O Neal; 27, ©Thinkstock/Fuse; 28cl, ©Shutterstock/Anita Peppers Patterson; 28cr, ©Shutterstock/App Stock; 28b, ©Shutterstock/Jasper Lensselink Photography; 29cl, ©Shutterstock/Vitalii Hulai; 29cr, ©Shutterstock/Cosmin Manci; 29b, ©Shutterstock/Xshot.

Brown Bear Books has made every attempt to contact the copyright holder.
If anyone has any information please contact licensing@brownbearbooks.co.uk

Manufactured in the United States of America
CPSIA Compliance Information: Batch #BS16PK: For Further Information contact Rosen Publishing, New York, New York at 1-800-237-9932

CONTENTS

Insect and Spider Machines

There are some machines that can leap many times their own length, make themselves 100 times heavier, and even produce flashes of light.

These machines are insects or spiders. The bodies of these bugs are living machines. They are equipped with moving parts, sensors, and a power supply, just like any mechanical machine. Insects, spiders, and other land invertebrates make use of a huge number of designs to survive in different ways. For example, an orb weaver spider produces super-strong silk for spinning a web; a flea can spring high into the air; and a tick is able to eat hundreds of times its own weight in food.

Myriapod: Centipede

Arachnid: Jumping spider

Insects, Spiders, and Relatives

INSECT	*	All insects have six legs and many can fly, using one or two pairs of wings; this is the largest group of land invertebrates
ARACHNIDS	*	Eight-legged invertebrates, which include spiders, scorpions, and ticks
MYRIAPODS	*	Land invertebrates with many legs; these bugs include the millipedes and centipedes

Insect and Spider Tech Spec

There are around one million different kinds of insects and 100,000 species of arachnids. They live in almost all land habitats, and they live in freshwater, too. However, very few survive in the oceans. Insects, spiders, and their relatives share these three basic characteristics:

* The body is surrounded by a tough exoskeleton, which protects the body and gives it its shape.

* The body is in sections: Insects have three, spiders have two. The legs are always jointed and made up of several sections.

* The temperature of insects and spiders is normally the same as the surroundings. This is known as being cold-blooded.

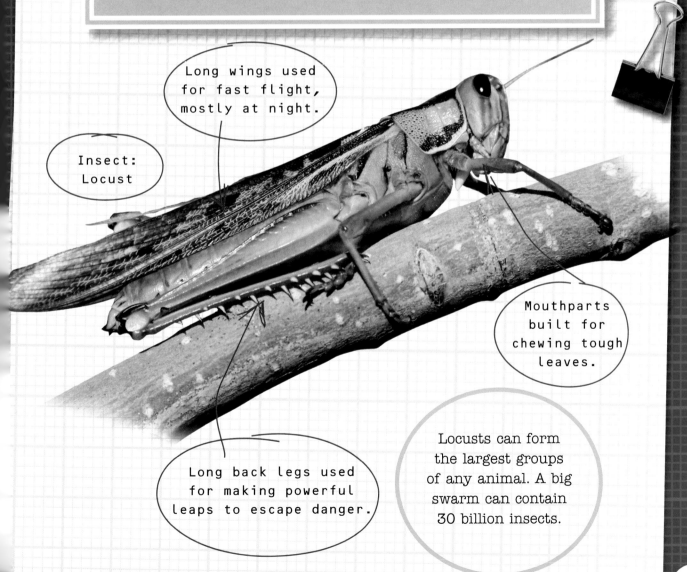

Long wings used for fast flight, mostly at night.

Insect: Locust

Mouthparts built for chewing tough leaves.

Long back legs used for making powerful leaps to escape danger.

Locusts can form the largest groups of any animal. A big swarm can contain 30 billion insects.

Leaf-Cutter Ant

UNDERGROUND GARDENER

Working in a team, these hard-working insect machines grow their own supply of food.

FACT FILE

Common name: Leaf-cutter ants

Length: 0.1–0.65 in (2.5–16 mm)

Color: red-brown

Where it lives: southern United States and most of South America; digs vast nests under the ground to depths of 16.5 ft (5 m); lives in colonies of up to 10 million ants

Food: fungus grown on leaf fragments

Predators: attacked by parasitic wasps and flies that lay eggs inside workers

Pincer mouthparts have sawlike edges for cutting tough leaves.

Profile

There are around 50 species of leaf-cutter ant. These ants cut up leaves and carry them back to the nest. They do not eat the leaves, but grow fungus on the leaves as they rot. The fungus produces rich fruitlike nodules, which the ants eat.

FAULT FINDER

The ants grow only one type of fungus. If another mold is brought into the nest, the ants must dig up the garden and throw it away.

WORKING LIFE

There are three main kinds of worker in the leaf-cutter colony. The smallest ants look after the garden; bigger ants cut and collect leaves; and the largest group, the soldiers, defend the entrances to the nest.

CLEANING	Bacteria grow on ants' undersides; bacteria make chemicals that kill all other fungi growing on the leaves
MUSH	Workers lick leaves clean and chew them into the mush that fungus grows on
SQUIRT	Fungus growth helped with squirt of liquid from the gardener ants' rear ends

Ants can strip a tree of its leaves in one night.

Teams of workers find the tree by following a trail of scent left by returning ants.

Worker ant can carry a leaf fragment 50 times its own weight.

TECH SPECS

The queen ant brings the fungus to the nest inside her stomach. She digs the nest's first burrow and throws up the fungus. She spreads it over cut leaves. Until the fungus garden begins to grow, the queen survives by eating her own eggs.

Tarantula

HAIRY DEFENDER

These big spiders have a special hair design that makes sure attackers leave them alone.

FACT FILE

Common name: Tarantula

Length: body 1–4 in (2.5–10 cm); leg span 3–12 in (8–30 cm)

Weight: 1–6 oz (28–170 g)

Color: normally dark, with red, white, and yellow patches

Where it lives: North and South America, Africa, southern Asia, and Australia

Prey: insects, worms, mice, and spiders

Predators: birds, lizards, small mammals, and snakes

Violent shake of abdomen fires off hairy darts. These stick into soft skin on lips and around eyes. The hairs get stuck and are very painful.

Hairs on eight legs pick up vibrations and chemicals from the surroundings.

Profile

There are 900 species of tarantula. The largest ones live in South America. They defend themselves with barbed hairs, which stick in an attacker's skin and cause great pain. Tarantulas from other regions have more powerful venom and use that for defense.

The tarantula's defensive hairs are covered in hooklike barbs. These grip the skin and make it hard to pull out the hair in one try. Barbed wire has many similar spikes. Anyone climbing over the wire normally gets tangled.

Eight eyes on top of head in four sets of two can pick up light, dark, and motion.

Fangs bite downward and pump in venom; venom is weaker than a wasp's sting.

Two shorter limbs called pedipalps are used for holding food.

Claws on feet are pulled in when walking.
* Speed: 1.25 mph (2 km/h)

STEALTHY HUNTER

The tarantula is an ambush hunter. It lies hidden in a burrow most of the time, only showing itself when prey comes close enough to attack.

TRIP LINE	Instead of a web, the spider spins long silk lines around the burrow; when prey touches one, the spider feels the movement
BLOOD POWER	The spider may have to chase prey; muscles bend the legs, but they are straightened again by pumping blood into the joints

Orb Weaver

MASTER BUILDER

This spider uses ultrathin stretchy strands of silk to build a lightweight but super-strong capture system. This design can trap a flying bug in midair.

WEB DESIGN

The type of web built by this spider is called an orb web. It is a flat web made up of spirals of silk hung between plant stems.

BRIDGE	The spider uses the wind to blow a silky strand across a gap to make the first line of the web
ANCHOR	A Y-shape of strands is hung from the bridge and connected to the ground to hold the web in place
FOOD STORE	When prey has been caught and killed, the spider may wrap it up in a silk bag and leave it for later

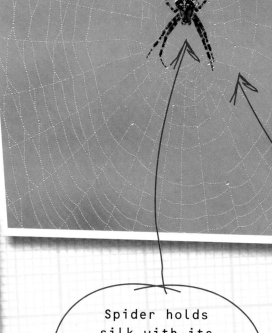

Profile

There are about 3,000 species of orb weaver spiders. They have a venomous bite for killing prey. Large spiders may bite people. The bites hurt but are not dangerous. Most orb webs are 2 or 3 feet (60 or 90 cm) wide. However, the bark weavers of Madagascar make webs that can stretch up to 80 feet (24 m) across rivers!

Spider holds silk with its claws and can feel the vibrations when prey gets trapped.

BIOMIMIC:

Orb weaver silk is the toughest silk produced by any spider. It is five times stronger than steel wires and can stretch four times its length without breaking. This silk may one day be used in body armor, sutures, and even as artificial muscle fibers.

Silk produced as a liquid. Gooey droplets are squeezed from spinnerets on the spider's abdomen. The droplets dry out in the air and are drawn into lines.

The spider moves around the web by standing on the nonsticky radial lines that lead out from the center.

The web is built across a flyway, a space between plants where insects fly.
* Build time: 1 hour

FACT FILE

Common name: Orb weaver spider

Length: body 0.25–2 in (6–50 mm); leg span 1–5 in (25–127 mm)

Color: mostly gray and brown, often with cream-colored markings or other colored spots

Where it lives: all over the world; in colder regions, most often seen in summer and fall

Prey: flying insects; the very largest species (golden orb weavers) may snare small birds very occasionally

Predators: birds, lizards, and snakes

A capture spiral of glue-covered silk runs out from the center of the web. Anything hitting the web gets tangled in these sticky strands.

Scorpion

The body design of this killer bug makes use of armor, sharp pincers, and a flexible stinger system for defense and attack.

ARMORED STINGER

FACT FILE

Common name: Scorpion

Length: 0.25–8.25 in (0.6–21 cm)

Weight: 0.2–1 oz (6–28 g)

Color: mostly a pale brown or yellow, but sometimes much darker

Where it lives: all over the world in warm regions; common in desert habitats but also found in rain forests

Prey: insects, spiders, and other small bugs; larger species sometimes catch mice or bird chicks

Predators: meerkats and other small hunting mammals, birds, and lizards

The tail can flex in any direction. It is usually curved over the body, holding the stinger ready to strike forward.

Eight legs used for running.

* Top speed: 12 mph (19 km/h)

HIDDEN FEATURES

ODORS	Detects chemicals on the ground using comb-shaped structures, called pectines, on the underside; males have larger pectines than females
GLOW	Body glows blue when seen in ultraviolet light; scientists think this is because of chemicals in the skin used to detect light

Profile

There are about 2,000 species of scorpion. They all sting, but only about 40 are dangerous to humans. Female scorpions do not lay eggs. The babies, known as scorplings, develop inside her body and are fed from her stomach. After birth, the tiny scorplings hitch a ride on their mother's back for the first few weeks.

Stinger is a hollow, clawlike spike that squirts venom into a target animal.

Two large eyes on top of head used for vision; smaller eyes on the side detect light and dark.

FAULT FINDER

Scorpions live alone and may attack each other when they meet. During mating, the male has to be very cautious about approaching a female.

Arms, or pedipalps, each have a pincer for grabbing prey.

Pincer is covered in touch-sensitive hairs, so scorpion can feel objects in the dark.

TECH SPECS

All scorpions are hunters. They chase prey and grab it with their pincers. Most kill their victims by ripping them apart with the pincers. Scorpions only use the stinger on large prey and for defense. The venom is too precious to waste.

Flea

SUPER LEAPER

This tiny bug has a big jump. It is built to live on the body of another animal, and it moves from one home to the next with enormous leaps.

FACT FILE

Common name: Flea

Length: 0.1 in (2.5 mm)

Weight: 0.0000353 oz (0.001 g)

Color: yellow and brown up close, but almost black when seen with the naked eye

Where it lives: worldwide, living on the bodies of mammals and birds

Food: fresh blood

Predators: spiders, roundworms, beetles, frogs, and lizards

Body is flattened so it can fit through the gaps between host's hairs.

Flea jumps off its knees; straightening the legs throws it into the air.
* Acceleration: 50 times more than space rocket

FAULT FINDER

Bites from a flea can spread diseases. The rat flea spread the plague by biting people. In the 14th century, the plague killed 60 percent of Europe's population.

Profile

Fleas are parasites, which means they live on another animal, called a host. There are about 2,500 species. Each species lives on one particular host (or perhaps a few), such as a rat, cat, or dog. Fleas live on their host for about a year, and they can lie dormant on the ground for several months without eating.

TECH SPECS

A flea can jump 7 inches (18 cm) high and make leaps 13 inches (33 cm) long. That is like a human jumping over a 14-story building and most of the length of a football field. The flea's leaping power comes from its elastic body. Before the jump, the body and legs are bent out of shape. As these spring back into shape, they flick the flea high into the air.

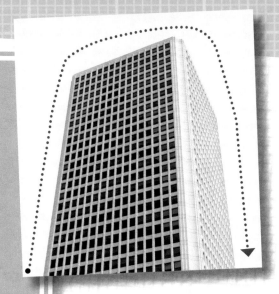

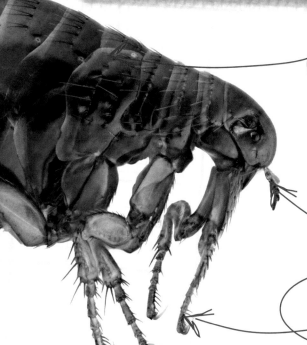

Hard plates cover the body. They are very stiff and protect the flea as it makes a crash landing.

Scraping mouthparts cut the skin. Flea then sucks up blood.

Claws on legs grab hold of the surface as flea lands.

SURVIVAL STRATEGY

A female flea lays 2,000 eggs in her lifetime. These fall to the ground, where they hatch into tiny wormlike larvae. Within 90 days, the larvae have become adults. The flea's amazing leaps are the way these wingless insects get onto their host.

COCOON	Larva transforms into adult inside case, or cocoon; young adult will stay in cocoon until it picks up the breath of a host; it then leaps onto it
HAIRS	Body has many backward-facing hairs, which hook onto host's fur

Dung Beetle

CLEANING UP

This tough beetle is built to survive on food that other animals produce as waste.

FACT FILE

Common name: Dung beetle

Length: 0.2–1.2 in (5–30 mm)

Color: black and dark gray

Where it lives: in all habitats worldwide except the polar regions

Food: dung of plant-eating animals of all kinds

Predators: preyed on by birds, lizards, and small mammals; parasitic wasps also lay eggs in the dung ball, so their young can eat the beetle grub inside

Beetle stands on front legs and pushes with its back legs.

Sawlike teeth on front legs used to cut and mold the dung into a ball.

TECH SPECS

Dung beetles search for dung while flying. When they pick up the smell of dung, they race to it. They need to get there before the dung has dried out and before other insects, like flies, have arrived and laid eggs in it.

BALL MAKER

Dung beetles need to keep their food safe from other beetles. They roll their balls away in a straight line because that is the quickest route to a safe place.

SIZE	Dung ball is never wider than the beetle's leg span; balls bigger than that would take too long to bury
MEASURE	While digging, the beetle measures the burrow against its outstretched legs until it reaches the perfect size

Egg laid beside ball. When grub hatches, it tunnels into the ball and eats it from the inside.

Dung formed into a ball and rolled away. It is then buried and eaten by the beetle.

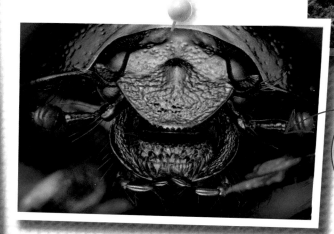

Frilled antenna is lined with odor detectors that pick up smells of fresh dung.

Fresh, damp dung needed so it can be shaped easily. * Ball is up to ten times weight of beetle.

Profile

There are 8,000 species of dung beetle. Some burrow under a supply of dung, taking their food with them. Other types slice off a chunk and roll it away first. Dung beetles make extra-large balls for their grubs to eat. The male and female work together to bury the ball, and the female lays an egg beside it.

Tick

BLOODSUCKER

This tiny bloodsucker does not get many chances to feed. So it has a design that allows it to eat many times its own weight.

FACT FILE

Common name: Tick

Length: before feeding, 0.12 in (3 mm); after feeding, 0.43 in (11 mm)

Weight: unfed, 0.0002 oz (6 mg); fed, 0.11 oz (3 g)

Color: brown, red, and black; becomes pinkish and white when swollen after feeding

Where it lives: worldwide, often found in damp places with thick undergrowth

Food: blood of land animals

Predators: frogs, insects, and birds, such as oxpeckers

Tick waits with its front legs outstretched to grab on to a host that passes by.

Tick detects approaching host by picking up the carbon dioxide in its breath.

Profile

The tick is an arachnid and is a tiny relative of spiders and scorpions. There are about 900 species, and all of them survive by sucking blood from a host. Most attack mammals or birds, and a few spread diseases.

Tick uses pointed mouthpart lined with many toothlike cutters. It uses these to dig deep through the skin to reach a blood vessel.

TECH SPECS

A tick only feeds three times in its life. Between each feed it molts, shedding its skin so it can grow bigger. After the third feed, the tick lays thousands of eggs and then dies.

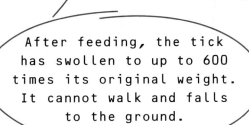

Only the abdomen and legs are visible as the tick sucks blood.

After feeding, the tick has swollen to up to 600 times its original weight. It cannot walk and falls to the ground.

BIG FEEDER

SALIVA	Tick's saliva is filled with an anticoagulant; this is a chemical that stops the host's blood forming a scab as the tick feeds
GUT	Instead of a tube, the tick's gut has many branches, which allow it to expand in all directions as it fills with blood
LEG COUNT	Adult ticks have eight legs, like all arachnids; however, tick larvae only have six

Honeybee

FOOD FACTORY

A honeybee is a busy insect that works in huge teams to make its own supply of nutritious food.

FACT FILE

Common name: Honeybee

Length: worker 0.4–0.7 in (10–18 mm); queen 0.8 in (20 mm)

Color: dark brown with yellow stripes

Where it lives: worldwide, except polar regions

Food: honey made from nectar collected from flowers; bee larvae and younger workers also eat mixtures of pollen and honey

Predators: bears, skunks, and birds raid honeybee nests; workers hunted by spiders and birds

Worker sucks nectar into a pouch called the "honey stomach."

IN THE HIVE

BEE BREAD	A mixture of pollen and nectar that is eaten by young workers; this food allows them to produce a substance called royal jelly
ROYAL JELLY	Powdery material is produced by the workers who feed the bee larvae that will grow into queens
DANCE	Workers tell other bees where to find flowers with a complex dance

Profile

Honeybees live in nests ruled by a single queen bee. Most of the queen's offspring are daughters called workers. The workers collect nectar and pollen, produce honey in the nest, and care for the next set of eggs laid by the queen. Every year, some eggs are grown into young queens and male bees, called drones, which fly off to mate and start new nests.

Cage-shaped spikes on legs used as "baskets" to carry sticky pollen back to the hive.

Worker bees store the food in hexagon-shaped cells in honeycomb made of wax.

Young honeybees (larvae) are reared inside honeycomb cells.

BIOMIMIC:

The six-sided cells of a honeycomb make it very strong and stiff while still being lightweight. Honeycomb-shaped materials are used by humans for the same reason, for everything from cardboard packaging (right) to the walls of spacecraft.

Firefly

NIGHT GLOWER

This bug's design includes an amazing component in the abdomen that can flash out light signals.

Profile

Fireflies are also called glowworms. This is because while the males have wings, the females do not and look like chunky worms. However, all 2,000 or so species of fireflies are neither flies nor worms. They are actually beetles! All adults can make light, and they use it to attract mates. The males begin the signalling; females flash back to show the males where they are.

LIGHT COMMUNICATION

The light from a firefly is used to communicate. Most species signal at nighttime, although some flash faint messages during the day as well.

EYES	Because they are so sensitive to light, the eyes of nocturnal species are blinded by daylight
RHYTHM	Every species has a unique rhythm of flashes so mates can identify each other
COLD LIGHT	Unlike electric light, the glow of a firefly produces no heat, only light

The light-making organ, known as the lantern, is in the tip of the abdomen.

BIOMIMIC:

Fireflies create light using a chemical called luciferin. This makes light when it is given energy by other chemicals in the cell. Glow sticks use this system. Cracking the stick mixes chemicals that work together to produce light.

The female firefly has the same body design as the larva. Unlike the male, it never transforms into a winged form.

The winged male finds a perch to signal to mates.

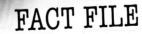

Lanterns of different species produce yellow, green, and orange flashes.

FACT FILE

Common name: Firefly, glowworm, or lightning bug

Length: 0.6–1 in (1.5–2.5 cm)

Color: females and young are brown or gray-black with red markings; males have brown and yellow stripes

Where it lives: worldwide in warm places

Food: females and larvae prey on slugs and insects; males eat pollen and nectar (or nothing at all)

Predators: birds, frogs, and reptiles

Stick Insect

This bug has the most extreme camouflage design of all. Its body looks just like a dried stick.

LIVING IN DISGUISE

FACT FILE

Common name: Stick insect

Length: 0.6–22 in (1.5–56 cm)

Weight: 0.02–2.3 oz (0.5–65 g)

Color: gray, brown, and green; often speckled to resemble wood and bark

Where it lives: worldwide in warm forests and woodlands

Food: most are plant eaters, feeding on leaves in sunny areas high up in trees; a few are hunters, preying on slugs and insect larvae

Predators: birds, frogs, reptiles, small mammals, spiders, and insects

The insect's long wings are folded along the body. The wings are often brightly colored, creating a startling flash when they are unfurled.

TECH SPECS

The stick insect adds to its disguise by rocking from side to side, like a twig swaying in the wind. If the bug is touched, it will fall to the ground and stay perfectly stiff and still, just like a dead twig would.

PLAYING TRICKS

EGGS	Eggs of most species look and smell like seeds; ants are fooled into collecting the eggs and taking them into the nest, which is a safe place for the stick insect nymphs to hatch
BUZZ	Wings are rubbed together to create a buzzing noise that scares away attackers
SQUIRT	As a final line of defense, a stick insect curves its abdomen over its head and squirts acid at attackers from glands on the tip

The head is tiny and has two small antennae. The largest features are the eyes, which the insect uses to find prey.

Profile

There are 3,000 species of stick insect. The scientific name for this type of insect is "phasmid." This is based on the same ancient word as "phantom." It refers to the way the insects can appear and then disappear from view.

Nodules and bumps, known as tubercles, look like knots, stumps, and flaky scraps of bark.

Some phasmids are disguised as leaves, not sticks.

Monarch Butterfly

This butterfly has a life plan that saves it from freezing to death in winter. It makes one of the longest journeys in the insect world.

LONG-DISTANCE FLIER

FACT FILE

Common name: Monarch butterfly

Length: wingspan 3.4–4 in (9–10 cm)

Weight: 0.009–0.027 oz (0.25 to 0.75 g)

Color: black body with white spots; wings are orange with black stripes and white spots

Where it lives: North America

Food: larvae eat milkweed leaves; adults sip nectar

Predators: few predators because the butterfly is protected by toxins

Adult monarchs fly south in fall to avoid the cold winter weather in North America.

The caterpillar eats its own weight in food every day for six weeks before transforming into an adult.

Caterpillar eats milkweed, a plant that contains a poison; the insect is unaffected and stores the poison in its body for the rest of its life.

In fall, monarchs from cold areas head south. They fly high (up to 11,000 feet, or 3.35 kilometers) to catch the wind. The journey takes several weeks. All monarchs gather in a few forests in Mexico and California and stay there all winter. In spring, the females lay eggs, and this generation of butterflies makes the journey north.

Millions of butterflies crowd into forest trees in the hills of Mexico. They stay there for four months without feeding.

Like the caterpillar, the adult is brightly colored to warn predators that it is toxic.

* Maximum journey: 3,100 miles (4,990 km)

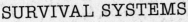

Perching prevents the butterflies from freezing. If one falls to the cold ground, it will freeze to death in minutes.

SURVIVAL SYSTEMS

BRUSHES	Butterfly has six legs, but only walks on four of them; the front pair are tiny and covered in brushlike hairs; the hairs are thought to be chemical detectors
SPIKES	Caterpillars have spikes at either end of the body; these confuse attackers, which cannot be sure where the head is
FAT STORE	Nectar drunk by adults is converted into fat to provide energy through the winter

MECHANICALS QUIZ

Now that you know more, test your knowledge of insects and spiders with this fun quiz. Answers on page 32.

1 Why does a firefly produce flashing lights?

2 Can tarantulas produce silk?

3 What does a dung beetle do with its ball of dung?

INSECT AND SPIDER RECORDS

HEAVIEST INSECT	giant weta 2.5 oz (71 g)
LONGEST INSECT	Chan's megastick 22 in (56 cm)
LARGEST SPIDER	Giant huntsman 12 in (30 cm)
FASTEST FLIER	desert locust 21 mph (34 km/h)
BEST JUMPER	froghopper 0.2 in (5 mm) long but can jump 28 in (71 cm)
LONGEST LIFE	queen ant lives for 28 years
DEADLIEST INSECT	mosquito kills 600,000 people a year by spreading malaria
DEADLIEST SPIDER	Brazilian wandering spider, South America

4 What does a tick feed on?

5 If a flea was the size of a person, how high could it jump?

BIOMIMIC:

Desert cicadas are able to keep their body cooler than their hot surroundings using an evaporation system. They fill channels on the outside of the body with water from the blood. As this water evaporates, it takes heat away with it. The same system is used in swamp coolers on the roofs of houses.

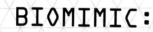

Glossary

abdomen The rear section of an insect or spider body.

antennae Feelers on the head of an insect; often used for smelling.

cocoon The case in which larval insects transform into adults.

elastic Able to change shape when pulled but always return to the original shape.

evaporate When liquid water turns into water vapor.

fungus A form of life that grows in the ground or over surfaces. Fungus absorbs food from its surroundings.

gland A body part that gives out chemicals; some glands are inside the body, while others, such as salt or sweat glands, are on the outside.

grub The larva of a beetle.

invertebrate An animal without a backbone; invertebrates include spiders and insects.

larva The young form of an insect that looks different than and lives in a different way than the adult form.

nocturnal To be active during the night when it is dark.

nymph The young form of an insect that has the same form as the adult and lives in the same way.

odor A smell.

parasite An animal that lives on or inside another animal, known as the host. The parasite does not kill the host but may make it unwell.

pedipalp An arm-like limb on the head of a spider or other arachnid.

predator An animal that hunts other animals for food.

prey An animal that is hunted by another animal.

radial Sticking out from the center to the edge.

saliva The liquid in the mouth; also known as spit.

sap The liquid inside plant leaves and stems.

species A group of animals or plants that look very similar and are able to breed and have young.

toxin A poison.

ultraviolet An invisible form of light that comes from the sun; creates sunburns and suntans.

venom A poison made by an animal that is injected into a victim using a bite or sting.

Further Information

Books

Burnie, David. *Bug Hunter.*
New York: DK, 2015.

Martin, Claudia. *Spiders and Bugs
Around the World.* Mankato, MN:
A+, Smart Apple Media, 2015.

Kovacs, Vic. *Spiders and Other
Animals that Make Traps.*
New York: Windmill Books, 2015.

Parker, Steve. *Insects and Spiders.*
New York: Gareth Stevens
Publishing, 2016.

Reynolds, Toby. *Insects and Spiders.*
Hauppauge, NY: Barrons Educational
Series, Inc., 2016.

Spilsbury, Louise. *Animal Bodies:
Extreme Anatomies.* New York:
Gareth Stevens Publishing, 2015.

Websites

PowerKids Press has developed an online list of websites related to
the subject of this book. This site is updated regularly. Please use this
link to access the list:

www.powerkidslinks.com/am/insects

Index

Answers to the Quiz:

1. To communicate with mates
2. Yes, for making trip wires but
   not webs
3. It buries it and then eats
   it or lays eggs inside
4. Blood
5. As high as a 14-story building

Off the Wall

The Art of Book Display

Written and Illustrated by
ALAN HEATH
American School in London
London, England

1987
LIBRARIES UNLIMITED, INC.
Littleton, Colorado

LIBRARIES UNLIMITED, INC.
P.O. Box 263
Littleton, Colorado 80160-0263

Library of Congress Cataloging-in-Publication Data

Heath, Alan, 1946-
    Off the wall.

    Bibliography: p. 145
    Includes index.
    1. Library exhibits -- Handbooks, manuals, etc.
2. Displays in education -- Handbooks, manuals, etc.
3. Bibliographical exhibitions -- Handbooks, manuals, etc.
I. Title.
Z717.H42   1987   022'.9   86-33792
ISBN 0-87287-578-4

Libraries Unlimited books are bound with Type II nonwoven material that meets and exceeds National Association of State Textbook Administrators' Type II nonwoven material specifications Class A through E.

For

Stephen, Pepper, and Pickle

my inestimable colleagues at the American School in London
whose creative environment has always inspired
innovation, experimentation, and personal development

the Hospital Hospitality House, Nashville, Tennessee,
for help during hard times

Beth Tidwell whose typewriter worked overtime

teachers in the many international schools in Europe
and around the world
whose enthusiasm for my work
has been an inspiration

Aidan and Nancy,
whose initial spark created this flame

TABLE OF CONTENTS

Part III
EXPANDING THE BOOK DISPLAY CONCEPT

INTRODUCTION

Displays speak to the individual reader at length, with humor or in seriousness, in vivid color and powerful images. They may move a reader to taste a book when more personal contact would fail.

Do we really fear that reading is on the way out? Perhaps not as much as we did back in the exploding 1960s when technology was really taking off. Today we accept that when a book is serialized on television or adapted for the cinema, sales and library loans of that book escalate. And most of us would argue that computers and personal videotape machines cannot replace the joy that books alone provide.

It is a mistake, however, to think that people in the book business—publishers, sellers, teachers, and librarians—do not have to compete with the color, noise, enthusiasm, and the excitement of Broadway to attract not just reluctant readers, but literate, busy people of all sorts. Publishers and booksellers have known this from the beginning. Didn't John Newbery offer free toys to buyers of his books in eighteenth-century London? But what happens to a book once it reaches a classroom or library shelf?

However attractive its cover or dust jacket, if the book isn't somehow thrust upon the reader, it may never move him or her to pick it up. Teachers and librarians, therefore, must use all the means at their disposal to move books, to get them off the walls and into readers' hands. No single means alone is enough. Book talks, bibliographies, and displays cannot suffice alone, but have to be used interdependently. Displays, though, are perhaps most important of all in that they are capable of speaking to the potential reader quietly and at length, humorously or seriously, in vivid color and powerful images, and may move a reader to taste a book when a more personal contact would fail.

This book, then, is about displays that have worked for me over a teaching career of nearly twenty years, both in the United States and in Great Britain. Some of them are very simple, while others are excitingly complex, and quite literally, off the wall. None is beyond the reach of anyone with scissors, pins, paper, and that illusive quality of the truly great chef—imagination. None of the following ideas should be copied without first adapting the idea to your own situation and environment.

This book is divided into three parts. The first part consists of three chapters that give the basic starting points: planning the display, design considerations, and materials to use. A section in chapter 2 describes the classic shapes in design that are generally used to set up displays of any kind. The classic shapes are presented boldface at their first appearance, for they are the basic layouts upon which many displays are built. Descriptions and display ideas are italicized when first mentioned, with lesser displays placed in quotes. The second part details several specific display themes, providing the particulars for accomplishing each one. The last part presents ideas for going beyond the simple book display, including displays to make with children and using displays as learning centers. Finally, a bibliography supplies not only further reading, but also a list of periodicals whose creative layouts may provide inspiration for the book promoter.

This book is not a "bible of design," but a handbook. Some of the ideas may not appeal while others will set off fireworks. Fireworks are, in effect, explosions. This book is about explosions of ideas which I hope will fill your display spaces and empty your bookshelves. Experiment with the ideas, materials, and methods which follow, adding, mixing, and adapting as you go until the recipe is truly your own.

The author hopes that *Off the Wall* will be useful not only to teachers, librarians, and others in the field of books, reading, and literature, but also to college and university students of education, children's literature, librarianship, and related disciplines. Because this book offers definite plans for several types of book displays, along with encouragement to adapt and change them, *Off the Wall* should stimulate discussion and action in courses such as audiovisual methods, the teaching of reading, public relations and advertising, and literature.

There is great joy to be had in uniting the right book with the right reader, and the joy to be gained through creative design in that happy process will, I believe, enhance our classrooms and libraries, and our careers as well as the lives of our readers.

HOW TO USE
THIS BOOK

Some books are meant to be followed as precisely as a drill sergeant on parade. This is not one of them. In order to illustrate certain general themes and ideas about the promotion of literature, a few specific displays that have actually worked are presented. In no way does this imply that they should be followed to the letter in every situation. In order to show the generalities, it has been important to deal with a few specifics.

Readers whose cultural and religious backgrounds do not allow them to celebrate Christmas, for example, must not take offense at chapter 5. The *idea* can be followed without any reference to the specifically Christian motif. A display relating to the Feast of Ramadan can be adapted from this one pertaining to the arrival of Santa Claus or Father Christmas. Behind each specific display lies an idea. It is that *idea*, and not how it took form at one particular moment, which is the true message.

For those who do wish, however, to use this handbook as a model, at least in the beginning, a simple *Grid System* can be made and applied to any illustration to facilitate its transfer to the display (see page xii). First, photocopy the illustration you wish to enlarge. Then, using a ruler and an artist's T-square or the corners of a five-by-seven-inch card to ensure that your lines are accurate, make a checkerboard grid over the artwork, dividing the surface into carefully measured squares. Each square will represent one arbitrary unit of measure, to be determined by the size of space available for the display. A square, therefore, could represent anything from five inches or less to several feet, and can aid in reducing or enlarging any piece of graphic work.

In recreating any particular drawing, copy the gist of the pattern or illustration. This will become quite easy after practice, even for those who insist they can't draw. Simply create a grid on your own paper in the same proportion as the grid on the original. Then redraw the illustration square by square. Some display artists will want to use separate pieces of paper to represent each square of the grid and then tape them together, tile-fashion. Begin anywhere with the drawing, but follow the illustration as it crosses each grid. Your copy of the original will cross *your* grid lines in approximately the same place as those on the pattern, thus giving you an enlargement in proportion.

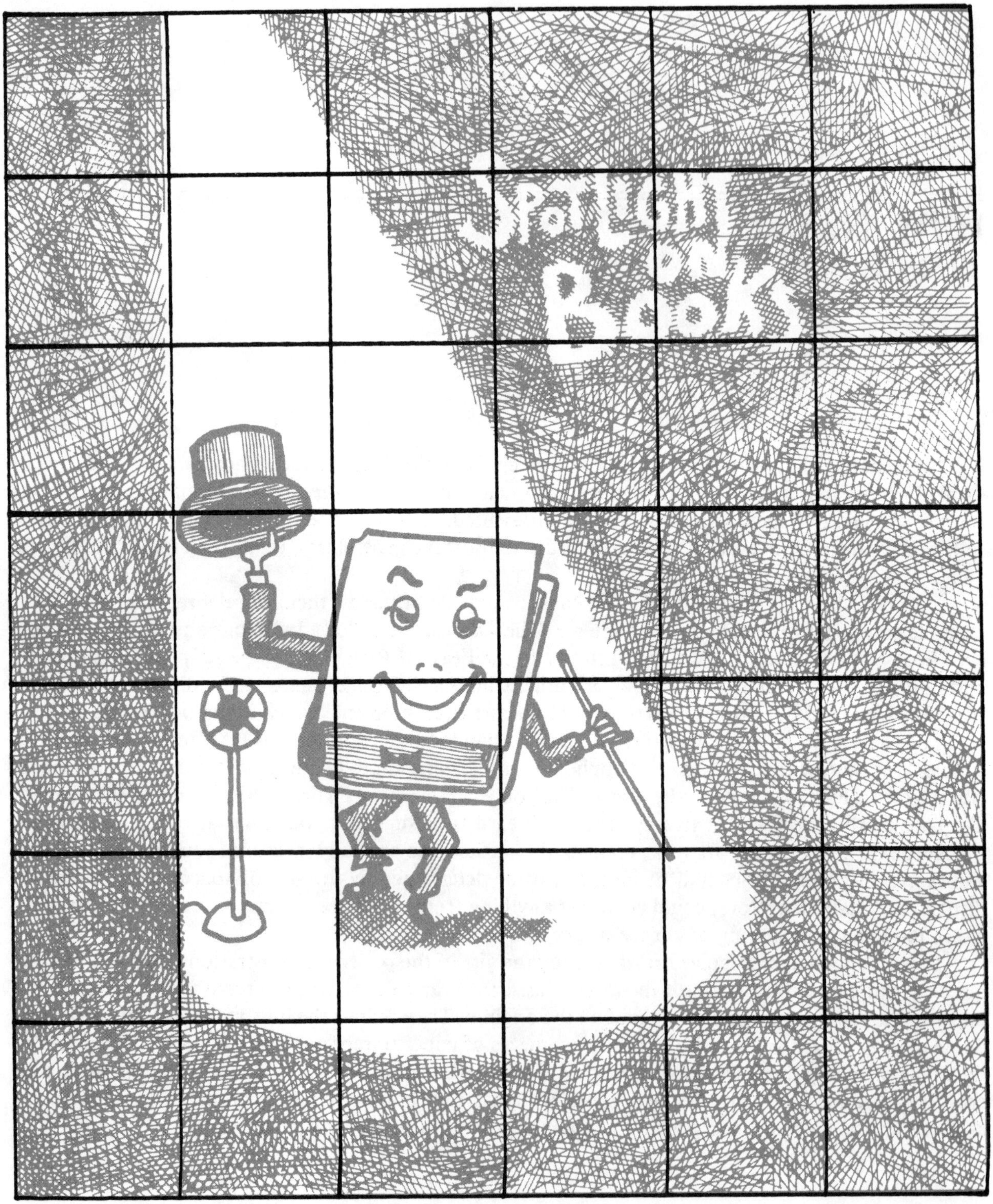
Spotlight
on
Books

Before copying any material from other sources, however, be certain to familiarize yourself with copyright laws to avoid embarrassment or a court case! When using photos or graphics from a copyrighted source, either obtain permission from the copyright holder (this should not be necessary if the display is meant to go no further than a classroom or school library), or give credit to the source in a small note at the bottom of the display. By changing the final drawing so that it differs drastically from the original, it becomes, in fact, your own work, as is the case with the examples in chapter 1, in which published photographs have inspired sports displays. Wholesale "lifting" of copyright material should be avoided, and it certainly must not be reproduced or distributed on a large scale without prior written permission. When in doubt, consult the copyright holder, who generally will not quibble with a non-fund-raising project, but will appreciate the courtesy.

The Grid System is not as complicated as it may sound. It does *not* have to be drawn out to size on one enormous bulletin board at once. What should be an enjoyable task would soon become a battle if that were the case. Students as young as nine or ten years of age have successfully made large murals using a variation of the Grid System. Each student is assigned only one grid which he or she then draws and paints as if it were a single piece of artwork. After all the students' work is completed, to a pre-specified size, they are all joined together in order. The results are often remarkably beautiful, with a shimmering quality which results from different brush strokes, color variations, and slight failures of lines to meet.

When the book displayer has put his or her grid together, failure of lines to meet exactly can then be corrected. The pieces of the grid can be taped together, and if appropriate, the large drawing can be cut out for use as a template for the colored paper illustration to be mounted in the actual display.

Another method of recreating graphic models and illustrations involves throwing the image onto a wall with an opaque projector or epidiascope. The major advantage is that the pattern need only be drawn once, directly onto colored paper, which has been taped to the wall. Also, the pattern can be projected to the size needed by moving the projector. Slides and filmstrips also can be used to create semioriginal artwork by projecting them onto a wall and tracing the outlines.

Still another method of reproducing drawings is to use the pantograph, available in good artists' supply shops for very little money. A pantograph is a set of flat, adjustable rods that will easily reproduce any drawing to a set scale with a bit of practice, though it is beyond the scope of this book to offer detailed instruction.

Most displays outlined in the following pages are made of commercially available paper. Schools will know it as construction paper, slightly more flexible than poster board, which can be too heavy for cutting with scissors and adhering to a wall easily. To offset the considerable expense of this colored paper, all of the displays are reusable and interchangeable, so that once made, they may be stored flat (in most cases) and brought out when required.

Other materials include cardboard boxes; cardboard tubes of the sort used to market paper towels, toilet paper, carpets, and fabric; newspaper; used tin cans (with rough edges filed down); cloth fabric; and coloring media: felt-tip pens, crayons, pencils, and watercolors.

Normally, scissors will be the strongest cutting tools required, although in some cases an artist's matt knife will be necessary. A stapler, drawing pins (or thumbtacks), cellophane tape, glue, and the occasional blob of Bostik Blu-Tak™ complete the basic tool kit.

For ease of reference, the following chart suggesting appropriate locations for some displays discussed in this book is presented here. Bear in mind, however, that even a helpful chart such as this may hamper your own creativity as you search for the right display for your own available space. Read on with an open, questioning mind.

Displays and Possible Locations

Materials or Title of Display	Page	Table	Floor	Shelf	Wall	Easel	Window	Ceiling
Don't Have Time to Read	3				X			
E.T.	3	X		X	X			
Tracing	4				X	X	X	
Lettering	12	X	X	X	X	X	X	X
Pegboard	18				X	X		
Interest Box	18	X	X	X				
Signboard	19	X	X	X				
Bookcase	20			X				
Pipe Organ	21	X	X	X				
Trees	24	X			X		X	
Son et Lumière	27	X	X		X			
Photographs	30				X	X		
Fox Box	32	X	X	X				
Book of the Day Poster	38				X	X	X	
Mobiles	38			X			X	X
Valentine	39	X	X	X	X			
Treasure Chest	49	X	X					
Santa's Pouch	61				X			
Santa Claus Trail	62				X			
Christmas Tree	64	X	X	X				
Easter Basket	68	X	X	X				
Tombstone	68	X	X	X	X			
Summertime	69				X			
Sail Away	71				X			
Discover Folklore	78				X			
Open Book	78	X			X			
Enchanted Forest	84				X		X	
Freestanding Animals	90	X	X	X				
Quip Strip Game	91	X	X	X				
Lilliputian Enchanted Forest	94	X	X	X				

Displays and Possible Locations, *Continued*

Materials or Title of Display	Page	Table	Floor	Shelf	Wall	Easel	Window	Ceiling
Pop-up	96	X	X	X	X			
Picture Book Gallery	100	X	X	X	X	X		
Space Odyssey	102			X	X	X		
Unicorn	103				X			
Dracula	103				X	X		
Spider Web	103	X		X				X
Spider	104				X		X	X
Stock Character								
face	106	X	X	X	X	X		X
body	106	X	X	X	X	X		
mobile	107							X
fairy tale	109				X	X		
Display for All Seasons	113				X			
Reading Tree	119				X			
Bookville	121	X	X	X				
Bookworm	130			X	X			
Flag	132	X	X	X	X	X		X
Banner	133	X		X	X	X		X
Activity Center	135	X	X	X	X			
Reader's File	136	X		X				
Posters	142				X			

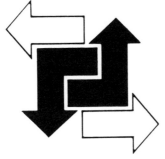

Part I Preparing Your Display

1

PLANNING THE DISPLAY

WHERE DO IDEAS COME FROM?

Ideas for new book displays occur everywhere. Book jackets are often good starting points. A newspaper advertisement may look just right for a display design. Often, photographs in newspapers and magazines easily translate into displays. If one gets into the habit of seeing life as one enormous tableau, display making becomes second nature.

Look at window displays of major department stores. Borrow ideas from them for your own situation. A sophisticated window dresser will not thrust a sample of everything available in the store into a display, but rather will select a few choice items to entice the prospective buyer. The best book displays, too, will not try to include every book available, but will select only a few. Some shops, especially the smaller "downmarket" ones, feel that they have to cram their display windows full of as much merchandise as they will hold, but the passerby cannot fix on any one item in the array. The same is true of book displays.

Look at the displays mounted by historical preservation groups, museums, or local civic authorities. The displays are inevitably free of unnecessary clutter; they are carefully and sequentially arranged; they are at eye-level; and they usually have something free for the observer to take away, such as a pamphlet, map, or bookmark. These ideas can be adapted very easily for book promotional displays.

To attract youngsters, keep an eye on current films and music trends. Capitalize on a popular movie by building a book display around the hero or theme: select some books for an extraterrestrial visitor, perhaps—and they need not be science fiction! A participatory activity could ask children to make a list of ten books they would want an alien visitor to read in order to get a better understanding of life on earth, its humor, tragedy, and daily existence.

A display that might attract adults could be entitled "But I Don't Have *Time* to Read!" Clip a few photos from magazines and newspapers of business people rushing about, of children watching television, of people preparing meals, etc., and then show a person—man, woman, or child—curled up in bed at day's end with a book. A concluding headline could read: "Some books for people who don't have time...." Below or nearby is a shelf of good reading, with books to be taken home.

The newspaper or sports magazine will prove invaluable in construction of a display to promote sports fiction. Look through the sports photos, especially the action shots, and clip the ones showing good body movement: a basketball player leaping for the net, a rugby forward driving toward the goal, a superb football kick. Place these photos on an opaque projector and enlarge them on the wall to create the outline for a good sports silhouette. Or make your own grid pattern so that you can enlarge it by hand.

Horses and other animals can be drawn using the same method: clipping from magazines and newspapers, enlarging, and displaying. Look in glossy magazines for photographs of houses to clip and enlarge. Also try the classified and small display ads for good graphics and lettering.

Another, rather old-fashioned, method of copying photographs, either from publications or from originals, is to hold the photo against a sunny window, beneath a piece of thin, white paper. Trace the outline of the character in the photograph and reduce all areas of gray to solid black. This creates a stylized, graphically exciting work of art that can be enlarged for a book display.

This method works well for those who deny their artistic potential to the point of saying bluntly that they can't draw. Nonsense. And for those who acknowledge their artistic abilities, the tracing method opens broader avenues of expression. The skier (figure 1a-b) first appeared in a travel agent's brochure. It captures perfectly the human body in motion and saves agonizing hours of freehand experimentation. The picture of the girl diver in figure 2 was produced from a photo of a gymnast in a European magazine. She could revert to that sport by removing the stylized water. Add a parallel bar, and she is in the gymnasium again. A hidden "extra" lies in store for those who trace, too: not only does the exercise create patterns to enlarge for a display board, it expands the tracer's knowledge of the human body, its movements and capabilities, thus moving the latent artist toward self-awareness and freehand expression.

Ideas stem from so many things that once they start flowing, they will perpetuate themselves. It will become necessary to keep a *file of ideas* lest they be forgotten. A scribbled note in a diary or on the back of a shopping list should be transferred to an index card and placed in a file-box for future action. The file also can contain newspaper clippings, advertisements, photographs, and other items that may be used later for book promotion.

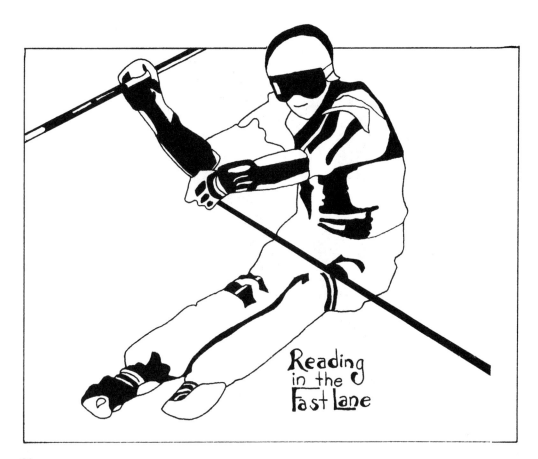

Reading
in the
Fast Lane

The top skier was inspired by a travel agent's brochure. Detail
was reduced to a minimum, with gray areas rendered in solid
black. Couple other skiers (Fig. 1b.) in a downhill race to promote
winter holiday reading.

Fig. 1a.

Fig. 1b.

Fig. 2.

A BOOK DISPLAY CAN FIT IN ANYWHERE!

Displays to promote reading will take time and effort, requiring forethought and several rough sketches. They may be truly grand in scale, covering not only entire walls, but floors, shelves, and ceilings, incorporating books, art, animals, cushions, spotlights, and a free drink. But before anything so time-consuming and energy-intensive defeats the incredulous, stop, take a deep breath, and start small.

To attract readers to the books it is not at all necessary to put up enormous acreages of poster paper and neon lights, nor is it essential to have that kind of space available. Make the most of what is at hand, whether it be a sunny interior wall, a tabletop, an old bookcase, or an unused corner. Likewise, do not despair if your display area is in a tired old building, with antiquated wiring and plumbing. Nor lament too loudly a meager budget, for most displays can use secondhand materials to a large extent and then can be recycled later on.

As you examine the many individual display ideas that follow, imagine how each one could fit into a space with which you are familiar. The examples in this book do not have to be reproduced exactly in your own space. They will need to be whittled down, rearranged, or molded to your own existing space. In one example, at least, the whittling has been done already—the fairly large Enchanted Forest, in chapter 8, has been pared down to a tabletop folding theater.

Try thinking of the least likely place for a book display, and put one there! Book displays are traditionally associated with libraries, bookshops, and classrooms. Why limit your creativity? What about the cafeteria, a waiting room, a trophy case, or the front hallway? Let the theme suggest the locale or vice versa: Halloween? A dark corner of the wasted space beneath a table might be perfect for the tombstone on page 68. Summer reading? A window would be ideal to attract outside passersby. The bookworm (page 131) could crawl down the hallway as easily as he could cross a classroom or library wall. Take displays to the readers, as well as expecting readers to come to the displays.

SEVEN THINGS TO DO FIRST

1. *Decide upon the Theme.* Rather than assembling a potpourri of diverse books, regardless of how attractive or well-written they may be, settle upon one central theme or mood which the display should convey. Instead of displaying merely "Good Books," put "Good Books for Summer Holidays" on show, or "Winners of Special Awards," such as the Caldecott or Whitbread prizes.

2. *Decide upon the Size and Amount of Space Available.* This may include a wall, bulletin board, table, shelves, floor, or an entire room. Determine the amount of time you have to spend on the display and the length of time the display will remain in the available space.

3. *Draw a Preliminary Sketch in Pencil.* Avoid frustration and disappointment by drawing a rough outline of how the display should look. If necessary, draw a floor plan or a map. Experiment with geometric shapes and arrangements of various elements of the design before translating the final idea to permanent (and perhaps expensive) materials. Take a lesson from interior decorators and cut out "dummies" to represent various elements in the display, such as posters, book jackets, artwork, and headlines. Move these about on the sketch or floor plan to see how various approaches will look.

4. *Assemble the Necessary Tools.* These may include paper; fabric; boxes; cutting tools; coloring media, such as crayons, pens, paints, and brushes; photographs, posters, and newspaper clippings; wastepaper receptacles; cloths and a basin of water; glue, paste, and tape; staples and a staple gun; drawing pins or tacks; and the books.

5. *Draw the Characters and Do the Lettering.* Determine the style of the characters and letters. Decide if artwork and graphics will be drawn, cutout, three-dimensional, or flat.

6. *Think about Storing the Materials.* Once the display has come to an end, will you be able to save most or all of the materials for future use? Do you have a storage system: cardboard boxes, file cabinets, closets, etc., arranged for easy retrieval of materials?

7. *Add Unused Items to Your Resource File.* You may not be able to use all the ideas you had originally assembled. In simplifying the display, you may have discarded some items. Rather than throw them away, store the unused items. Write down the ideas for later use.

2
DESIGN AND ILLUSTRATION CONCERNS

TITLE OR HEADLINE?

Generally speaking, displays should always have a headline; that is, their titles should have old-fashioned subjects and verbs. Even if it proves necessary to spend considerable time waiting for the right verb to come bouncing along, come it will. And the display will be all the more useful for it.

Instead of calling an attractive Christmas display "Christmas Reading," make it dynamic with complete sentence construction, for example, "Skate Away with Our Christmas Reading!" or "Santa's Mad about These Books!" Of course, the design would have to coordinate with the headline. It would be silly to depict the Madonna and Child with one of those titles. Something more subdued would be appropriate, but again with a subject and predicate: "Hodie Christus Natus Est," though unintelligible to many, is certainly more celebratory than "Christmas Reading."

Think of other seasonal and topical displays. Instead of shaping up a really good Dracula on the display board and ruining it with a weak title such as "Halloween Books," put some bite into it with "Join the Count in Some Ghastly Reading," "I'm Bats about Books," or "Put Some Bite into Your Reading." If you happen to be pushing dog books, don't dampen your reader's spirits with a bland title."Read about Man's Best Friend" or "Read One of These to Your Dog Tonight!" is more alluring. A St. Valentine's Day display could be headed, "Big-Hearted Books Improve Your Chances."

Snappy headlines should be short, sweet, and to the point. Borrow the filmmaker's jargon, and make a sign that says, "You Saw It on the Silver Screen—Now Read the Original!" The display could include every book in reach which has ever been made into a film. Substitute "TV" or "Cinema" where appropriate, and include a drawing or silhouette for added interest.

There will be times when a title may be better, but any display will be weakened if a subject and verb are not used.

CLASSIC SHAPES IN DESIGN

Before designing, cutting, stapling, and pinning, it is a good idea to look at some classic shapes in periodical layout and design, for they illustrate perfectly what is pleasing to the eye through attractive use of space. An issue of *Better Homes and Gardens, In Britain,* or any other colorful, good quality, illustrated magazine will be the perfect companion to this exercise, for they use each of the following patterns in making their pages at once dignified and attractive (see the "Bibliography" on page 147).

Rather than slapping a bit of paper here, a picture there, and some writing elsewhere, try designing your next display around one of these rather formal seven layouts: the Clothesline, Townscape, Pinwheel, Dominant Element, Mosaic, Isolated Element, and the Sketch (see figure 3). Not only will they help to structure ideas, but they will also enable the display viewer to get the point quickly.

Using a popular periodical, locate a layout which uses the **Clothesline.** This may take the form of photographs, drawings, or a combination of the two with text and headlines, in which all elements have a common top margin. It does not matter about the bottom limits of the various elements. That they terminate at various distances from the top makes the layout more exciting to the eye and relieves the boredom inherent in too regular an arrangement.

A first cousin to the Clothesline is the **Townscape,** in which all elements share a bottom margin. Note that in a display one of the elements may be text, surrounded by posters, drawings, or book jackets, and the text may be hand-lettered on poster paper or cut out from fabric or paper. In the Townscape, or Skyline, the irregular top margins not only provide interest, but space for a headline or two.

A favorite layout arrangement with teen magazines is the **Pinwheel.** Don't expect to find a layout exactly like the archetype shown here, but watch for similar ones. Usually there will be a series of four or more photographs or other elements revolving around a central imaginary point, rather like a child's toy pinwheel. Their position around the point creates visual motion, so that the eye sweeps around the circle continually.

Perhaps a publishing house has provided a large poster about one of its authors, or a large map or travel poster may be available that could form the **Dominant Element** of a display. Look for related posters, such as book jackets, photographs clipped from old magazines, children's drawings, or your own artwork, and arrange them around the dominant element in a **Mosaic.** Sometimes it is difficult to tell whether a design is Pinwheel or Mosaic, since they share some common points, notably the effect of dancing or swirling movement, but the Mosaic usually contains many small elements around one larger one.

For the beginning display artist, it may be tempting to describe first attempts as Mosaics, but if they are true Mosaic layouts, all elements will have equal space between them. There will not be large gaps between some and narrow ones between others. See how the best-illustrated magazines handle this excellent technique. Look on the walls of good art galleries also or in the homes of people with an innate sense of attractive design. Paintings will be grouped together as units, with the same margins or gaps between each frame, not scattered on the wall as if they were flung there. Mosaic display layouts, too, will function as single units, providing they are well-thought-out before mounting.

A variation on any of the above themes involves the **Isolated Element,** in which one part of the display calls direct attention to itself through intentional and careful displacement. Normally the isolated element will be a large poster or photograph, related to the display, but worthy of special attention. It must be far enough removed from the rest of the unit so that it is obviously not a mistake, but it should be connected to the larger unit graphically, perhaps by a narrow line or border running full length above or beneath the other elements and bleeding off both margins. This graphic line can run beneath the isolated element or run all around it to make an attractive border and to further

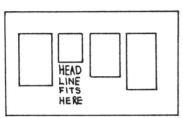

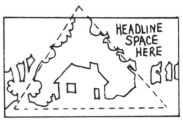

The Clothesline, in which all elements share a common top line. The headline should fill space as if it were a piece of artwork.

The Sketch, in which collage, drawings, or other art forms combine in irregular shapes, usually around an imaginary triangle.

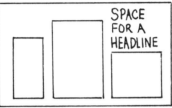

The Townscape, in which all elements share a bottom line, with headline filling space as if it were a solid area of artwork.

The headline in The Sketch may be placed in any unfussy open space.

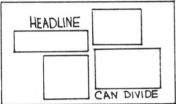

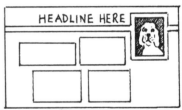

The Pinwheel, in which all elements swirl from an imaginary point in the center. Headline should rest on top of an element, dividing if necessary to another part of the display.

The Isolated Element, in which one important object receives special treatment, while being connected to the rest of the layout by graphic lines.

The Mosaic, in which all elements fit like a puzzle. Outer margins unimportant, but inner margins must be the same. A Dominant Element is just off-center.

The headline usually fits along the graphic line that unites the Isolated Element to the layout, which may be any Classic Shape.

Fig. 3.

separate and call attention. The headline usually fits perfectly above or beneath this graphic line.

A favorite display shape, however, is the **Sketch,** for it is not limited by rectangles, circles, or formal parameters. Magazines rarely use this one, and if they do, it normally takes the form of one large two-page spread photograph, with some textual matter inserted in an unfussy corner, burned onto the photo. The Sketch lends itself not only to walls and bulletin boards, but also to windows and mirrors (see chapter 8), allowing the artist to use his full potential.

There are some boundaries, however, within which the Sketch operates best. Normally, the Sketch evolves around an imaginary triangle or some other shape. The triangle, a soothing, calming shape, tranquilly unites various elements into one whole by directing movement back upon itself. Above all, the Sketch encourages the use of all forms of creative paper art, from cutting and bending into three-dimensional shapes, to drawing, painting, and collage.

None of these shapes is to be regarded as absolutely authoritative, for there are always exceptions to the rule, just as there are always extraordinarily unusual places into which displays can fit, places that may prove to be unique. The classic shapes, however, are tried and true. They clarify tentative or hesitant approaches to display by those whose experience is limited; they are sophisticated, easy to look at, and simple to do. In short, they work.

LETTERING TECHNIQUES

Designing the lettering for displays often can be one of the most creative aspects of the task, but beginners may very well shudder at the idea of turning out beautifully formed alphabets. To start, if you do not wish to create your own letters, buy commercially available stencils or templates from a good educational supplies dealer or from an art shop. Then all that remains is to trace them, cut them out, and put them up.

If you use a template, however, trace the letters backward; that is, turn the template onto its reverse side before copying so that you trace the letter backward. This not only gives your scissors more scope in cutting around difficult corners and curves, but more importantly, the finished letters will be free of the telltale tracer's mark. Turn the backward cutout over, and you have a letter of professional quality with your pencil guidelines unseen on the reverse.

To improve the quality of cutout curved letters, move the hand that is holding the paper, guiding the penciled letter into the cutting blades, and keep the scissor hand steady. The result is a smoother curve, free of choppy or irregular cuts. Practice this technique especially on the letters O, Q, P, S, B, C, G, and U, and on any curved shapes in more extravagantly designed alphabets.

Before designing original alphabets, it is best to examine a few methods of displaying the letters (see figure 4). In addition to putting letters straight onto the display surface, it is quite simple to hang them from the ceiling, thus creating displays in midair, or to make shadow boxes to call more attention to the message.

Flat lettering is the simplest way to apply cutout letters, which are stapled or pinned to the board or glued to paper, usually in a straight horizontal line, so that they lie flat against the background. They may be applied directly onto the display background or given emphasis by being glued to a contrasting sheet of paper.

Raised lettering is the close cousin of flat lettering, for flats are raised against their background using straight pins to hold them away from the surface. In even casual room lighting, this creates a natural shadow and movement.

Basic shadow box lettering requires only one patiently designed set of flat characters glued onto one large sheet of different colored paper. These are then cut from the sheet, leaving a margin around each letter, roughly in the shape of the original. This process can be repeated several times, for once

1. FUN

Flat lettering is the simplest to cut out, and is the basis for all other variations.

2. FUN

Basic shadow letters begin life as flats. They are glued to another sheet of paper, and then the display artist cuts around them, leaving a border in contrast.

3. FUN

Simple Shadow Box lettering requires two of each letter. The twin letters are fixed at a diagonal, one over the other.

4. FON FUN

Shadow Box lettering requires two of each letter, but these are attached to each other by a "bridge", folded on the dotted lines, and suspended from the ceiling.

Attract readers by suspending all or part of the heading in front of the display.

5. FUN FUN

Suspended lettering requires a top flap, or tab, which can be folded back and taped or pinned to the ceiling in front of a wall display.

Fig. 4.

the first set is cut out, they can be glued to yet another sheet of paper of a different color and cut out again. This is a good job to give a willing assistant.

The result is a set of very colorful and attractive letters. Rather than choose just any colors, try to set a decorative style. Make the original set in black, for instance, and glue them to white paper. Cut them out and glue them again to black. Place the black-and-white letters on a gray background. Or use varying shades of one color. Or create a rainbow, using a patchwork of colors, gift-wrapping paper, grocery bags, or whatever is available.

Simple shadow box lettering creates the illusion that each letter casts a shadow on the background. To achieve this, cut out twin letters, preferably in different colors, placing one atop the other, diagonally, on the display surface. To cut out more than one letter at once, staple no more than two sheets of paper together around the edges and also between the traced letters, if possible, for stability. Holding the paper firmly, cut slowly, taking care that the two sheets do not slip. It may be necessary to add a few more staples as you move down the line to provide further stability. Simple shadow box can be combined with raised lettering for added drama.

Joined shadow box lettering may become a favorite means of making decorative alphabets, but this method requires considerable patience, at least at first, and plenty of time, always. Begin by drawing the required letters. Then, depending upon their size, extend the top lines of the letters upward on the paper for approximately two or three inches. Any further than this and they will become unwieldy. Then, at the top of this "extension," draw mirror images, using stencils or templates, so that when you have finished, you have two rows of letters, one atop the other, separated by two to three inches of connecting paper strips. When you cut them out, fold the tops of the letters so that they form right angles with the connecting paper and you have instant shadow box letters. Attach the letters to ceilings with tape or pins or to bulletin boards in the usual way.

These joined shadow box letters have the pleasing quality of moving in a slight breeze, and provided that the connecting strip is not too long, the front letters dangle slightly lower than their shadows. Experimentation with several grades of paper will probably convince you that ordinary construction paper is best, for it is light enough to allow the front letters to dangle as if on a string, it cuts easily, and it is the same color on both sides, an important consideration.

Suspended lettering can animate a bare patch of ceiling in a most unexpected way and is easier to make than joined shadow box letters. This method hangs well on porous tiled ceilings, for a straight pin placed at an angle through the letter and into the tile assures a simple but secure bond. Plaster or wooden ceilings can also take suspended letters with tape or Blu-Tak™, but the bond may not hold. Suspended letters resemble joined shadow box letters in that they also have the connecting bit of extended paper at the top. It is this intransitive flap which is adhered to the ceiling, leaving the letter to sway beneath. Suspended letters can be very dramatic, especially if they are quite large, even up to three feet in length. And they look very good hung a foot or two in front of the rest of the display.

Some letters provide interesting problems, particularly when they are large or if the paper is too thin. The worst letter of all is *S*. Its bottom upswing has a mind of its own, and without precautionary action, it will resemble a snake after only a few moments in the air. All is not lost, however, for there are at least two ways of correcting this. The first, and in some lettering styles the only means, is the attachment of a length of string or thread between the upswing and the body of the *S*. Normally the string is not noticeable once the letter is suspended (see figure 5).

The other method requires that you design an alphabet which will cope with and overcome the problem naturally, and results are stunning. This method could rightly be called the *Brunell* since it makes use of "girders," much as the famous British engineer might have used iron girders to support his bridges. Ornate Edwardian-inspired alphabets lend themselves to bridging girders (figure 6), which support awkward letters, such as free-swinging *S, E,* or *M.*

To support a large "S" attach a fine thread to keep the letter from "flagging".

Fig. 5.

Build in support with "girders." These integral pieces will prevent "sagging".

Fig. 6.

To achieve individuality and character in homemade lettering, try copying letters from book jackets, which often reflect the flavor and local color of the book itself. Do this freehand with the grid method, enlarging the letters to suit the display. Photocopy the dust jacket, draw a grid pattern across the lettering, and proceed to enlarge. If you don't feel confident with this, or if the results you have achieved are not entirely pleasing, use an opaque projector to help trace the letters on the wall.

Copying from book jackets will be especially helpful if you want character letters for pseudo-Chinese, Greek, Cyrillic, Hebrew, or others in various national styles. Your imagination is the only limitation. Indeed, imagination is often the only way to fill in the gaps when a book jacket doesn't provide all the letters you need for the headline in the display. It will not be too difficult to build missing letters from parts of others: *E* can become an *F*, and vice versa; *O* makes a *Q, C,* or *G; L, T,* or *R* makes an *I; P* is nearly an *R;* and so forth.

A good experiment for those who maintain artistic innocence is the construction of a *Neanderthal Alphabet* (see figure 7). Start by marking off a simple geometric grid on plain paper. Then, using the squares of the grids as a guide, make a capital *I,* one square wide, and at least three squares long. Proceed to the more difficult letter *T* by extending the top of the *I* by one or two squares on either side of the top. While these may be perfectly good cutouts as they are, roughen them with scissors as you cut them out and capitalize on the imperfections. Dig in an extra gouge here and there, allowing the scissors to stray from the pencil line, but not too much.

Using the grid which you have made, make the other letters of the alphabet so that they are of uniform height and thickness. As you cut them out, make nips and tucks with the scissors, rounding off corners in letters which require it (such as *R, S, C, P,* etc.). Even the first results should be good enough to use as templates, and by saving all subsequent letters, you can build up a fine reserve. By careful reuse, future workloads can be reduced, so that drawing and cutting time can be spent on other things.

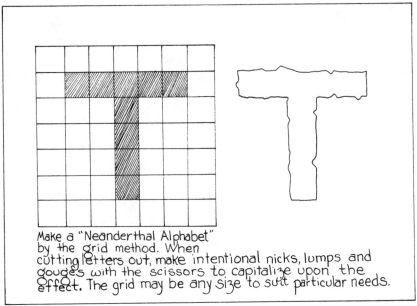

Make a "Neanderthal Alphabet" by the grid method. When cutting letters out, make intentional nicks, lumps and gouges with the scissors to capitalize upon the effect. The grid may be any size to suit particular needs.

Fig. 7.

THE ILLUSIVE STRAIGHT LINE

After conquering the template and scissors, producing an attractive set of letters, there is the nasty problem of putting them up in a straight line across the bulletin board or display. To avoid drawing an unsightly pencil line across the display (which may look even worse if you attempt to erase it), use one of these methods.

Pin-and-String. Determine where you wish the letters to appear, and measure from the top of the first letter to the ceiling or to the top of the display area or other point of reference. Stick a pin at the edge of the board at that height. Stick another pin on the other side of the board at the same height, and tie a thread or string tautly across the space between them. This thin line will guide you as you place the headline across the display. Remove the string and pins upon completion.

Cutout Templates. To place headlines in semicircles or other nonhorizontal shapes, avoid the unsightly pencil mark by cutting a template to the required shape. Staple or pin this to the bulletin board and place the letters next to the shape. Templates may be made by drawing around upturned wastepaper baskets, dinner plates, barrels, or by using pins and tightly pulled thread to make sharp geometric forms.

To make a semicircle or circle, place a pin on a sheet of paper. Attach a string the length of the required diameter, and to the other end of the string, tie a writing tool, a pen, pencil, crayon, or chalk. Using the pin as the center of the circle, stretch the string tightly, and slowly swing the pencil over the paper around the pin. The result should be a fairly perfect circle.

Resist the temptation to place the headline vertically, especially if the letters themselves are to be positioned horizontally (figure 8). If it is absolutely essential to use the stylistically outmoded, hard-on-the-eyes arrangement, at least place the letters on their sides, so they can be read from bottom to top.

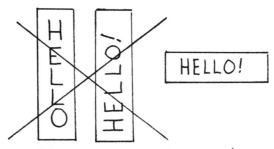

Always display letters horizontally.
Any other arrangement will be
too difficult to read.

Fig. 8.

3

MATERIALS TO USE IN DISPLAYS

USING BOOKS TO SELL THEMSELVES

Although the best book displays don't necessarily include books, they may be included occasionally. In school there are some obvious drawbacks to using books in displays — the purpose of the display is to circulate reading matter, and if a book is on a display rack or shelf, it isn't being read; if readers are encouraged to remove the books from the display, then gaps occur from time to time which may not be readily filled; and it is unthinkable to encourage the public to read a book, at the same time refusing them permission to do so since it is "on display." There are some ways around these difficulties, however, which enable the display to continue while its books are being read.

Thematic displays representing genres of literature with large collections on hand certainly can use books as visible focal points. A display encouraging the enjoyment of science fiction, for instance, can have as its core a group of from fifteen to twenty titles, with the attached proviso that "YES! You *can* take these books!" As soon as a John Wyndham is removed, it can be replaced with a John Christopher or a Poul Anderson until the supply is happily depleted.

As many ways exist to display books as there are shelves, racks, pegboards, and readers, so even a lengthy study of these means will not be definitive. It won't hurt, though, to observe a few trusty displays with books at the core to see how they can be adapted to the space on home territory.

The *Pegboard* is an easy device to exploit, since tall books, fat books, tiny books, and skinny books can easily look their best together there. Also, pegboards can be entirely covered over with poster paper and the "pegs" discreetly fitted into their holes so that the books hover in a display larger than the board itself. Pegboards often appear in school hallways, bookshops, libraries, classrooms, and dining areas, so all that remains is to display the books — with covers on show, a benefit not always associated with standard library shelving.

The *Interest Box* is good for a tiny space, such as a table or desk and concentrates a few topically related books into a handy container, literally a box. Any grocer's box will do, turned on its side, so that the books can be viewed as if in a bookcase. Students often enjoy making the decorations for the box, especially when older readers prepare the display for younger cohorts. One drawback, however, is that the book spines, and not the front covers, are on show.

Any books with a related motif can be used: leaving home, school life, teenage problems, animals, or literature about the American frontier. The Laura Ingalls Wilder *Little House* series (New York: Harper & Row Junior Books, 1973), *Miss Hickory* (New York: Viking, 1946), *The Matchlock Gun* (New York: Dodd, Mead & Co., 1941), and *The Yearling* (New York: Scribner's, 1983) can live happily in a Frontier Box. In a pouch glued to the side of the box could be an assortment of activities which readers can do, either for enjoyment, enrichment, or for a mark in the teacher's book.

An advantage of the interest box is that books on many different reading and age levels may be collected and made available to readers. Thus, adults or teenagers may pick up *The Matchlock Gun,* an award-winning picture book, to enjoy it for its superb artistry as well as its historically significant story. Similarly, young children may take home *The Yearling* long before they can read it for themselves, for an older brother or parent to read aloud to them.

The *Shelf* is an all-too-obvious place for displaying books, but imagination often overlooks the commonplace. Bring a bare space to life with an impromptu shelf built up of castoffs from the lumberyard placed on top of brick risers. Or stack some fruit-packing crates on top of each other sideways to create a colorful display area, especially if the crates are painted a bright basic color, such as red, yellow, or green. Add a doll or two dressed in period costume, put up a title or headline, and a few words of explanation, and there is an effective exhortation to the would-be reader.

Make self-supporting signboards to dress up the shelves by folding a rectangular piece of heavy card into three equal widths (see figure 9). Make these folded pieces into a triangular column, taping the ends together to make the sign sturdy. Another fastening method is to leave a tab or flap at one end that can be folded into the signboard out-of-sight and taped internally. These little signs can be used to direct readers to what they're looking for among the bookshelves or to highlight special collections.

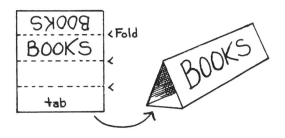

Fig. 9.

The *Table* provides an accessible display area, especially for books intended for immediate handling and sampling. Two bookends to support the upright books and space for a more casual spread of books across the table, and the display is ready, with perhaps a small signboard or two to set the theme. Desks and study carrels can serve this same purpose. For adults, a pot of hot coffee and biscuits would not be at all inappropriate here either.

The *Floor* is also a prime space for displaying books. Young children are accustomed to playing, reading, and listening to stories on the floor, where books, toys, and cushions are accessible. Book displays can also claim the floor for older readers, especially when display stands of varying heights create visual movement from the floor up to table height or beyond. Packing cases can become book stands, some of them placed on end, others on their sides. Likewise, bricks, or even stacks of books, can be used to display single volumes.

To add sophistication to a floor display, lengths of fabric can be draped over the stands to hide what might be unsightly (or at least uncoordinated) boxes and bricks. It pays to look for fabric remnants, but hessian (or burlap) is a fairly economical alternative that has the advantage of textural blandness and continuity, focusing all attention on the display of books. Fabric has a long life, which is a bonus for book promoters who will want to use it again and again.

The addition of a few pillows and a chair or two makes the display totally inviting. Large floor cushions are inexpensive and comfortable, not to mention fun, and encourage the browser to curl up with a book. And who really minds if someone falls asleep before the end of chapter 1? A potted plant will also make the area less utilitarian, as will a small scatter rug, a table lamp, or a few objet d'art of a sturdy nature. The floor brings books and book displays down to a living level, within easy and comfortable reach, which is just where books ought to be.

DUSTHEAP TO DISPLAY: PROMOTING BOOKS WITH CASTOFFS

Aunt Mary has finally sold her house in the country in order to retire to Majorca, and fortunately you remembered that large bookcase in the parlor, claiming it just before the antique dealer swooped. Perfect for your book display, and best of all, free! Mrs. Flimwell, the newspaper seller, has just thrown out a wire-frame paperback rack, the kind which kids love to rotate on the ball-bearings but which drove poor Mrs. Flimwell around the bend. She never oiled the wheel. At night, with Aunt Mary's bookcase still on the roof rack, you drive by in your best disguise and salvage the discarded bookstand from the dustheap. Perfect for your book display, and best of all, free!

Pilkington's, the elite haberdashery and department store on Balmoral Square, has just filled an entire skip with used window-display materials: wooden fences, paper shrubs, and a flock of fairly dirty papier-mâché pigeons. Following the raid on Flimwell's, you salvage these goodies from the fate which awaited them. Perfect for a book display on summer reading, and best of all, free!

The amount of waste in the western world is not only alarming from an ecological point of view, but also from an economical one, too. Book people often have little funding for the promotion of their material to readers, so it behooves us to be on the lookout for throwaways from shops and homes. Naturally, it may be preferable to ask the management's permission before taking anything, for this common courtesy may open the avenue for further benefaction. Once the manager knows of the local book promoter's need, he will probably be very happy to give advance notice of discarded shelving and display materials.

Be on the lookout for other sorts of salvage, too, such as cardboard boxes and tubes from factories, crates from shops, wood remnants from lumberyards, even books from classrooms, schools, and libraries. If petty cash has a few coins therein, a trip to the junk merchant or secondhand shop may enrich a future display with a cheap desk, shelf, or artist's easel. In short, an eagle eye will detect all manner of usables in unlikely places, from rubbish heaps to family attics.

An old bookcase makes an ideal vehicle for displays. If room is available so that it does not have to be packed full of books, library-fashion, the bookcase can be an upright treasure chest. Line the back of the case with attractive material, such as shiny metallic paper, fabric, or colorful paint. Then put books onto the shelves as if they were fine china on exhibition, with attractive paperback covers and dust jackets arranged to catch the readers' eyes.

Borrow an idea from the architects of those baroque Austrian churches when giving the display a title (figure 10). "Good Books for You!" may be too general, but it fits a miscellaneous collection and looks good on a swag. Just as the baroque artists used cherubs to hold ribbons, arrows, flowers, and other garlands, the modern display artist can use angels, animals, or cartoon characters to hold up the festoon. The bookcase lends itself to other signs as well. Hang a sign from the ceiling near the bookcase which says "Reading Matters," a double entendre in the very best sense. Intersperse a small sign or two among the books (figure 11) for these little placards not only relieve the pictorial assault of the book covers, adding textural relief and interest, but if a drawing or cutout is included, the message gains humor and impact.

Fig. 10.

Potted plants are visually attractive on bookshelves, creating a natural, homelike atmosphere. In book displays, however, the soil in the pot is usually wasted space. Surprise browsers by putting a little placard on a stick in the flowerpot. Stuffed toys, dolls, trains and cars, and other paraphernalia will also make the shelves more interesting. But let the books themselves be stars of the show by limiting the placards and objects to a few choice pieces.

Cardboard tubing, of the sort around which fabric and paper is rolled, is a byproduct usually relegated to the debris depot. And that's where it should stay, thinks the busy book promoter, unaware that this rich resource can be shaped into pipe organs, tree trunks, pencil cases, and bookshelves.

To celebrate Christmas, Easter, or a music festival, install a pipe organ over a low table on which are placed some seasonal books, and just watch the merry browsers helping themselves! "But surely a pipe organ is unreasonably difficult," exclaims one who has never collected cardboard tubing while whistling "The Holly and the Ivy." Not only is the organ simple to build and easily storable, it is visually surprising and sufficiently unusual to attract interest.

The pipes will be less likely to fall over if they are housed in a case, which can be cut from a cardboard box. The box serves to reassure the wary book promoter, too, since only two rows of pipes are needed to simulate the instrument rather than several freestanding ranks. Design some large decorative openings in the front of the box to expose the pipes to view (figure 12). Use Gothic windows as a thematic inspiration, or design others to your taste, seeking Victorian steam organs and calliopes for ideas. A word of caution, however, is that simple curves and straight lines are much easier to cut from cardboard than baroque convolutions.

To create a realistic illusion, it is better to have several sizes of tubing, from tiny to enormous, but don't despair if variety is limited to toilet rolls and paper toweling; when they are painted, the tubing will look authentic enough. Fill the front of the organ case with pipes, beginning on one end with short, skinny ones, graduating to tall ones in the middle, and sloping down the other side in similar gradation. The next row should be done in reverse, but using thicker tubing if possible. To make rows of pipes less apt to fall, glue or tape them into a cardboard trough which can be fastened to the bottom of the case (figure 13). Cutting the tubes to size is best done with a sharp matt knife. To cut a straight line, thereby rendering both parts of the pipe usable, mark a point at several places around the circumference at the same height from the bottom. Connect the points with a pencil line, and slowly run the matt knife along it.

A simpler rank of pipes may consist of one row only of identical tubes, rising to the top of the case. This uniformity is still quite realistic, since many small chamber organs of the eighteenth century look like this, but it is less interesting in the cardboard version. To secure the front row of pipes to the case, place double-sided tape or glue along the bottom and top of the box front. Insert the pipes,

Book shelves and potted plants serve double duty when they carry signs to encourage reading.

Fig. 11.

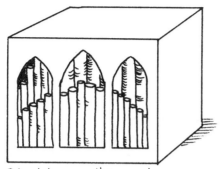

Simulate a gothic or baroque pipe organ case by cutting out appropriate openings in a cardboard box. The pipes are empty rolls from paper towels, foil, and toilet tissue.

Fig. 12.

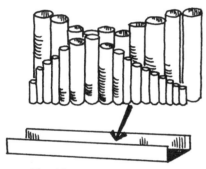

Place the pipes in a trough made from card. Glue the pipes to each other, as well as to the trough. Then position them inside the organ case, securing them with tape and glue.

Fig. 13.

packed as tightly as the box will allow, and encased in the trough, which may have double-sided tape or glue on the bottom. To add further strength, secure each row with a single length of cellophane tape, running horizontally near the top of the shortest pipes from one side of the case to the other.

To save time, spray paint the pipes and case. Many Victorian organs have gold pipes in a wooden case, which the paper organ can simulate, either with paint or paper. For duotone, it is necessary to paint the pipes and the case separately before joining them together.

A keyboard can be made from another cardboard box (figure 14), preferably a fairly thin one, which can be laid on its side. Keys need not be in high relief, with raised black notes, but they can be made from small pieces of wood and glued onto the white notes or simply painted on. Organ stops can be successfully simulated with cotton thread spools, 35mm photographic film canisters, shampoo bottle tops, or other small cylindrical containers. The case for the keyboard should be painted the same color as the pipe case.

Place the finished organ on a low table covered with paper or cloth. Arrange seasonal or thematic reading matter casually on the surface, interspersed with decorations appropriate to the season or festivity: artificial greenery of paper or plastic, Christmas tree ornaments, a pot of spring daffodils, other musical instruments, sheet music, carnival or circus posters, or stuffed animal toys.

A scroll can be made to fit across the pipe case to extend appropriate greetings or to title the display. "Make Merry with a Good Book" is a jolly Christmastide headline. "Pipe Down and Read!" could be a pun too illusive, but might make boisterous young readers see the displayers' sense of humor.

The assembled pipe organ includes a simulated keyboard painted onto another box, a canopy made from two cardboard "gables" and poster paper, and stops made from 35 mm film canisters and spools of thread.

Fig. 14.

Cardboard cylinders also can be turned into stylized tree trunks and branches. Depending upon the height of the display, trunks can range in size from kitchen roll cylinders to linoleum rolls. They can be cut in half lengthways and used flat-sided against the wall; used whole, they can be adapted to become freestanding.

Cardboard tubes make excellent conifer trees (figure 15), which benefit from the straight lines of the trunk. To make it freestanding, place the tube in a trough or flowerpot of clean sand, or follow this easier indoor method: measure one and one-half inches from the bottom of the tube, marking all around the circumference with a pencil. Then divide the segment into four parts of roughly equal size. With scissors or matt knife, separate the four parts and fold them back. Flatten them as much as possible, and further subdivide the quarters with other incisions if necessary. Glue them to a piece of heavy cardboard and secure with staples or tape.

Greenery to cap the trunk can be made from a sheet of stiff green paper, folded into a cone and glued, taped, or stapled together. Make a cone by cutting a semicircle from the paper, then folding it gently around until the sides of the diameter slightly overlap. Additional texture may be added by gluing strips of fringed paper over the conical structure, overlapping rather in the manner of roof tiles, but if the display is to contain a forest, this extra effort may be too time-consuming. Place the cone on the top of the cylinder, the crest of which has been generously bathed in glue.

To make young conifer trees, eliminate the cardboard tube. Place paper cones of varying sizes around the adult trees. This further simulates a forest, especially when small cardboard animals, cottages, and paths are added (see chapter 8).

Tubes can be added to wall displays, too, though there may be problems when it comes to fixing them securely in an upright position. To make tree trunks, cut the tubes in half from top to bottom, leaving two fairly perfect troughs. These can be fastened to the vertical display with clear tape, preferably with a matt finish so that it isn't too obvious.

Leaves can assume several stylistic arrangements. To make an oak or maple, cut cloudlike masses from stiff paper. To continue the three-dimensional texture, place supports beside the trunk and behind the leaf mass so that they will be raised from the display board. Supports can be made from one short strip of stiff card, folded four times into a "tunnel," then stapled to the vertical display beside the trunk at strategic points (figure 16).

Two trees made from paper foliage glued to empty paper towel rolls, and placed in a pot of sand. Glue two leaf masses to each roll, one on both sides.

To enable the tube to stand without a flower pot, make incisions around the base. Fold them back and tape securely to flat surface.

Fig. 15.

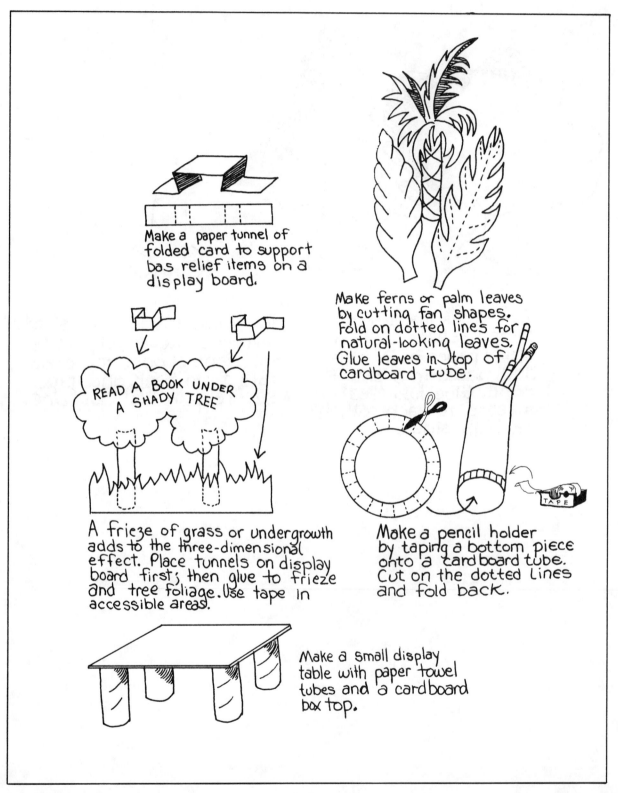

Make a paper tunnel of folded card to support bas relief items on a display board.

Make ferns or palm leaves by cutting fan shapes. Fold on dotted lines for natural-looking leaves. Glue leaves in top of cardboard tube.

READ A BOOK UNDER A SHADY TREE

A frieze of grass or undergrowth adds to the three-dimensional effect. Place tunnels on display board first; then glue to frieze and tree foliage. Use tape in accessible areas.

Make a pencil holder by taping a bottom piece onto a cardboard tube. Cut on the dotted lines and fold back.

Make a small display table with paper towel tubes and a cardboard box top.

Fig. 16.

To make palm trees, cut leaf strands individually from appropriately colored paper. Cut a large fringe into the feather-shaped leaves, or cut indentations to give the impression of palmate formation. Leave a stem at the bottom which can be glued into the top of the tube. When the palm is fully leaved, bend some of the strands down over the side of the trunk, allowing others to remain upright. The trunk can be decorated with diagonally criss-crossing lines to simulate the peculiar pattern of the palm.

Blend the rather abrupt high relief of the tube trunk into the rest of the display by making a grassy foreground of paper to place over the area, supported by cardboard tunnels. Depending upon the theme and type of literature on display, the foreground can also contain fences, meadows, undergrowth, flowers, animals, or buildings.

Cardboard tubes also make pencil cases, bookmark holders, and pots for artificial flowers. Determine the height needed, and carefully draw a line around the tube at that level. Then slit the tube apart with a matt knife. Make the bottom from a piece of rugged paper, cut to fit and taped into place; jam jars may be easier, but cardboard tubes won't shatter if they accidentally take a tumble. To make the bottom, place the upright tube on the paper and draw a circle, about one-half inch larger than the width of the tube, around it. Also trace the shape of the tube itself in the center of the larger circle. With scissors, cut carefully from the edge of the piece of paper to the inner circle to make flaps. Glue the flaps to the inside of the tube, or tape them to the outside. If the latter procedure is used, it will be essential to cover the tube with colored paper, both to disguise the taped flaps, and to protect them from wear and tear.

Simple bookshelves can be made easily from large, sturdy tubes. Determine the height needed, and follow the procedure for making a pencil case, but don't make a bottom. When there are at least four tubes, turn them upright onto the corners of a cardboard tabletop. If the shelf is very much over eighteen inches long, place additional tube supports in the middle. Fasten the tubes to the cardboard shelf or table with incised flaps (as in the conifer tree), which can be glued, taped, or stapled. Turn the unit onto its cylindrical legs, and it should support a fair number of paperbacks or a few small hardbacks.

Make several of these shelves in various widths and heights to use in floor-level displays, to give texture to tabletop displays, and for variety with upturned packing crates. Cover the tops in colored paper. Turn the cylindrical legs into candy canes by applying narrow strips of red paper over white paint. The shelves won't last indefinitely, but their easy construction and low cost counterbalance a comparatively short life.

INCORPORATING SOUND FOR AN AUDIO DISPLAY

Book displays may be static, carefully choreographed around a single theme, quietly urging the reader to dip into the ordered rows of paperbacks at his disposal. Or displays may shout, reach out, and grab the eyes and ears of passersby, forcing them to stop and pay attention. Consider, therefore, the humble cassette tape recorder: cheap, widely available, and easy to use. Make it work for book promotion just as it does for the music industry by creating a talking display.

The *Son et Lumière* approach is especially effective with younger readers who will enjoy listening to what the tape has to say; and that, of course, is up to the book promoter, who may choose to record a story or a fragment from a longer book, preferably one which will be part of the overall display. The recording could feature a dramatic reading, based on one of the books, or it could even be a "radio play," with several voices portraying the characters in the book. It is feasible to augment the audio with some attractive visuals, such as slides of students dressed up as the characters.

The cassette recording should be fairly short, from ten to fifteen minutes at most, so that (1) the listener's interest will not waver, and (2) the listener can move on from the tape to the exploration of the books, giving another listener a chance to hear the tape. It probably will be preferable to require the use of earphones so that others will not be disturbed by the tape. Up to four or more headset users could listen at once, depending upon the space and sound system available, and still have room to touch the books comfortably in the listening and display area.

If the tape features a dramatic reading done by a good storyteller, either the display artist or a talented colleague, the story must be clear, theatrical enough to lift it beyond the ordinary, and should reflect the reader's own personal enjoyment of it. The choice of story depends largely upon the person who does the reading; it must be a story which he or she can read well, which has been rehearsed many times, and which can be communicated with enthusiasm to others.

The cassette recording captures the story more or less permanently; it can be used long after the display has been removed for storage. Over the years, it is easy to build a library of recorded stories to use (1) in similar displays; (2) when it is not possible to read stories aloud to a group; and (3) individually with headphones during quiet reading times. A classroom or library can put up a *Listening Post* for individuals to plug into whenever appropriate. The rest of the class could be doing other activities while the listener is enjoying the story with headphones.

Personal experience has shown that a school's turnover of pupils allows a librarian to reuse display materials, whether audio or not, in direct ratio to the frequency of students' movement to higher grades. For instance, if a lower school includes grades one to four, and you have made a Listening Post display for the top two grades, you can use it again, as new, when both of those grades have moved on to junior high school, and then set a pattern of using that particular display once every three years. Teachers of a single grade or age level can, of course, reuse their display materials again each year, for their turnover occurs annually.

To produce an adaptation of an original piece, the book promoter has in effect to write a radio play with script, possible sound effects, and different characters, which may be done by the same person using different "voices" or by a team of readers. The radio play, again, has to be short to be most effective among youngsters whose natural curiosity may lead them to other things in the middle of a long tape. Lengthy productions could be divided into segments to avoid overtaxing the patience of young listeners. They enjoy the "tune in same time, same station" approach, anyway, if the display requires serialization.

A variation on the radio play which children themselves can do quite successfully takes the form of the radio talk show. This may be used in place of the more conventional "book reports," making the less literarily inclined feel more comfortable with writing. Using the format of the radio chat show, the students select a host, a team of "celebrities," and perhaps an advertising announcer or two, since it is often easier to entice the uninterested scholar with the prospect of advertising Bow Wow Dog Food. The show could be called something very bookish, such as "St. Trinian's School Book Review Program," "Our Top Ten Books," or "Have You Read This?" That sets the theme right away, so that the children know exactly what the show is about. The host is responsible for writing his introductory remarks and for introducing the celebrities, which is considerably less involved than the task in store for *them*.

The celebrities must rearrange their thoughts about the typical book report by first asking themselves several questions:

1. Why did I (not) like this book?

2. Why were the characters believable (or not)?

3. Why was the setting (not) important?

4. Why would I (not) recommend this book to my friends?

5. How does it compare to other books on the same theme?

6. Why is this book (not) relevant to today's reader?

7. Why is this book (not) better than the film of the same title?

Then they must write their comments on these topics, which, with other relevant questions, will become the body of the show. To speed matters, the celebrities should write down the questions which they themselves want to be asked, along with their answers, so that the host and the adult in charge can assemble them into a flowing script.

Several celebrities may have read the same book, and the tape can be a discussion of one author's works. Or they each may have read different books. The host should be familiar with most of the books, too, for he or she may come up with some probing questions that the celebrities may have overlooked. The adult in charge should not try to stifle controversy or differences of opinion about a book, for honest appraisals in discussion may stimulate intellectual growth among the participants and their listeners.

The chat show can be introduced with theme music, and, if desired, a humorous ad can be thrown in. Better yet, advertise an upcoming school or community event, such as a play, concert, or ball game. Very little should be left to spontaneity lest awkward silences degenerate into embarrassing giggles. The show can close with well wishes from the host, enjoining listeners to pick up copies of the books at the library or from the display itself as the theme music begins to play. The show should last no longer than ten minutes when made for inclusion in the book display, although longer ones may be desirable when they form part of a class project.

A sophisticated sound system is not necessary to make a good cassette recording. Good results can be achieved with a simple portable recorder, a cassette tape, and a microphone, which may even be built into the machine. Participants must be careful not to rustle their papers, make unnecessary noises of any kind, or tap their fingers or pencils on the table. Sound effects personnel can work with a record player and a record, turning it on at the right moments, and fading away with the volume control button. The recording should be done in a quiet area, free from ticking clocks, school bells, and street noises, with a notice posted outside the door to prevent the curious or the unwary from bursting in.

When the tape is completed and ready for the display, place the cassette recorder on a desk or table with the appropriate books nearby, either on a pegboard, the tabletop, or shelves. A catchy title, such as "Hear What the Celebrities Have to Say," or "St. Trinian's Radio on the Air!" should invite listeners to pick up the headsets and turn on the recorder. Precautions to be taken include instructions for use of the recorder, including rewinding for the next listeners. These can be written on a small placard posted near the machine. The recorder should be fixed so that the tape cannot be erased or recorded over, either by accident or otherwise.

It may be unnecessary to make an elaborate wall display to go with the chat show if the books and the tape are powerful draws. A photograph of the production team would be a good idea, though, especially if they are holding copies of the books which they review in the script. A subheading or title could induce listener participation by asking passersby to "Join host Antony Blodgkiss on St. Trinian's Radio Top Ten Books Program! Today he talks to Melissa Brown, John Reader, and Teddy Booker. Brought to you by Miserable Morsels, the unlikely dog food!"

Along similar, though more complicated, lines, adults and students can work together to produce videotaped book programs as well. In many schools, a television monitor may be available for a book display. There are few youngsters who dislike television, and a homemade program, with local host and celebrities, will attract plenty of attention. Some may argue that the medium will overpower the message, and that too much work will go into a project with little literary outcome. Others will rightly find out that a good videotape can put the "o-o-o-o" back in books!

USING PHOTOGRAPHS OF READERS TO PROMOTE READING

If any display in this book is guaranteed to work, it is this one, which uses photographs of children to encourage others to read (figure 17). If placed in school, be prepared for parents to come in to see their child's photo. If placed in a public library, shopping center, or any other place where books are promoted, expect a similar interest from parents, friends, and the curious who want to look at the photos. They may even go away with the books.

One of the classic shapes in design (see page 10) will lend itself admirably to the photographic display, for maximum visual impact requires neatness of form and definition of space. Simplicity, too, is essential, for any hint of fussiness will detract the eye from the clean lines and order of the background paper, photographs, and text.

The thesis of the photographic display is rather like that of some famous advertisements in which a celebrity praises a particular television set, wine, or tennis racket. By endorsing the product, the celebrity makes the ordinary man and woman want to buy it. Similarly, even in a humorous vein, local "celebrities" can endorse their favorite books in an attempt to win new readers.

Fig. 17. This variation on the classic Clothesline design achieves clarity through interdependence of text, headlines, and visuals.

Begin by selecting a few people who wouldn't at all mind being photographed for public display and who can write a few words to recommend a book. Then all that remains is to take and develop the pictures, add the celebrities' comments, and attach them to the display area.

A carefully selected title will enrich the visual impact of this essentially simple display. Perhaps "The Best Book I Ever Read" is too direct, but it is certainly eye-catching in bold letters against a somber background. Include the name of the school or library or shop with such titles as "St. Trinian's Readers Recommend ...," "Get It at the Sleepy Hollow Library!" or "Bookshoppers' Best." Or try "The People Read," or ask, "Read Any Good Books Lately?"

Obviously, it is better to take photos with a good 35mm camera, but don't despair if your talent extends no further than an inexpensive fixed-focus lens. Black-and-white film will achieve more dramatic results, but color is perfectly acceptable. If cost is a concern, then do use black-and-white film, especially if enlargements are to be made.

Vary the styles of the portraits. Photograph some subjects with the book which they recommend. Photograph others reading in a comfortable chair, checking out the book from the library, or reading aloud to a group of listeners. Include some ordinary mug shots, especially of the more dramatic types. It may help if a plan of the proposed display is at hand when the photographer is at work, for then the photos can be made to fit into the overall design. On the other hand, excellent photographs may inspire an entirely different layout from one's original plan, such is the serendipity of this project.

If the display is to be seen from a distance, say from across a large room or lobby, use only a few large photos. But if the display is intended for an intimate corner, use one or two dominant pictures with a cluster of smaller photos alongside. The rule of the-more-the-merrier will work in some displays, especially in schools when everyone will want to see himself or herself and friends in the display.

Some guidelines should be given to the celebrities before they write their short book recommendations. Youngsters may need only the encouraging word, for few will write in length. Older readers may need precise instructions, giving them a "twenty-five words or less" framework.

A certain charm occurs when the celebrity's actual handwriting appears beneath his or her photograph, but to speed viewers through the display and on to the books under consideration, it is better to rewrite the recommendations in a standard form. Press-on lettering is ideal for this, but could be time-consuming and very expensive. Most typewriting will be too small. Cutout lettering will probably be too large and would certainly take more time. Careful rewrites with felt-tip pen on pieces of paper cut to size to harmonize with the photos will give the best results.

An interesting sideline will inevitably result from this photographic display, so keep the negatives handy. Parents will want to buy copies of their children's portraits; sweethearts, grandparents and friends may well want to purchase also. A discreet notice placed beside the display might state that copies of the photos are available, and that proceeds will benefit further book sales for the local library. Profits also could be diverted to a dwindling promotion budget!

A bookmark bibliography that recaps the display will be a semipermanent reminder to the viewer who doesn't have time to get the books he wants immediately; he can take the bookmark for future reference. If funds permit, make a bookmark for each celebrity, printed on stiff card complete with photo, comment, bibliographic information, and the name of the sponsoring organization, perhaps with opening times and other pertinent facts.

Add variety with a few group photographs in which all members of a class, team, or governing body (such as a town council) endorse one or more books. In school, a homeroom or class could discuss the books they have read to come up with their top five favorites. The photographer captures the students for all eternity, and once *that* photo goes up on the wall, stand back to give the viewers room! If fifteen kids are in the picture, then a guaranteed audience of fifteen will bring five times that number. Even greater success may be had when the football or soccer team is cajoled into a similar promotional photograph.

Public libraries can use this idea to promote their entire collection, rather than a few particular books. A display in the town hall or in a shopping center, with photos of local citizens and their comments about the library, reading, and good books, will produce good public relations, and new patrons may emerge from casual passersby.

USING PUPPETS TO SHOWCASE BOOKS

Like many ideas which grew out of unlikely situations into successful ploys, the *Fox Box* evolved over a two-week period at the opening of school one sunny autumn. To compete with the unseasonably hot sunshine outside, it was necessary to grasp the children's attention (and the teacher's!) with a variety of stimulating activities, including the introduction of a new puppet who literally stole the show at story time and eventually became the closest thing the school had to a mascot.

This puppet was (and still is) a beautiful handmade fox, who sometimes served as an Uncle Remus character or took on other roles, depending upon the situation. That one fateful day, he was merely "Freddie" and spent the first few minutes of the story session "asleep" in a nearby cardboard box, out of sight of the children.

While the students were getting acquainted with each other and their teacher, talking aloud about the books they had read over the summer and about the ones they would take home that evening, the teacher called for quiet in a rather shocked, professorial voice. At first the children thought they were being reprimanded, but soon they fell into the drama enthusiastically.

"Shh, did you hear something?" demanded the teacher. Intense quiet. "Listen, I think I hear it again!"

"What? What did you hear?" asked one particularly inquisitive girl in the front row.

"I thought I heard something scratching. Listen! There it is again!"

"Yes, I heard it!" volunteered a boy on a cushion at the back. "I heard it!"

At this point, the teacher thought that his magic might be working after all! It was time to call attention to the box, a plain one with colored paper covering. "I think it's coming from inside this box," the teacher said, placing the box on his lap. By now, the children were ready for anything, their curiosity and involvement evident in wide eyes and open mouths.

Cautiously, the teacher opened the lid of the box and exclaimed, "Why, look at this! How did *you* get in here?"

"Who is it? Let me see! What's in there?"

Slowly a red ear presented itself to the children, then a black nose. This was greeted by simultaneous cheers, gasps, and a certain amount of applause, which, of course, frightened the fox back into the box, giving the teacher the opportunity to explain how shy the creature was and that he must have quiet if he is not to be frightened away. That also gave the teacher a chance to place his left hand firmly inside the glove puppet.

It was discovered that the fox had brought a book along with him, which he and the teacher then read to the class. Later in the week, Freddie Fox was joined by Cedric the Bloodhound for a Russian tale about a wily fox and his walking stick. This time, both puppets went to the willing hands of two children seated on the floor beside the teacher's rocking chair. The spontaneous mime accompanying the story was marvelous.

Soon, Freddie and Cedric were joined by Nelson Bear and Pete, a rather handsome, rustic hare with long ears and an exquisite white tail. Again, the animals each brought exciting news for the children in the shape of another storybook; each story was acted out by several students as the teacher read the tale.

The puppets were so popular that many students asked if they could visit them during their lunch breaks and during other periods of free time. Almost without exception, each visit was accomplished with remarkable decorum, and included original drama, storytelling, and sharing of books with the puppets and other children.

It soon became evident that the puppets needed a better home than the open shelf to which they had been relegated, so Fox Box evolved from a mundane cardboard carton into a fairytale cottage, fitted with window shutters, a door that opened and closed, and a removable roof that permitted access to a well-decorated floor and walls inside. Fox Box took about two hours to build, but with adaptation could take far longer, depending upon the imagination of the builder. Like many successful book displays, Fox Box began simply, with an ordinary cardboard box. The tools were simple, too: scissors, a matt knife, glue, a straight edge, pencils, felt-tip pens and colored paper.

To make a similar house, either for dolls or for puppets or stuffed animals used with storytelling and creative dramatics, choose a cardboard box such as those used to package photocopy paper, canned vegetables, or books. It should be about fifteen inches high and twelve inches wide. Draw a sketch of the house first, determining where the door(s) and window(s) will be. Experiment with extra touches, too, such as flower boxes, a porch roof, chimneys, and shutters. Sketch in the details of door facings, curtains, and bricks and stones. When everything seems right, then start to work on the box (figure 18).

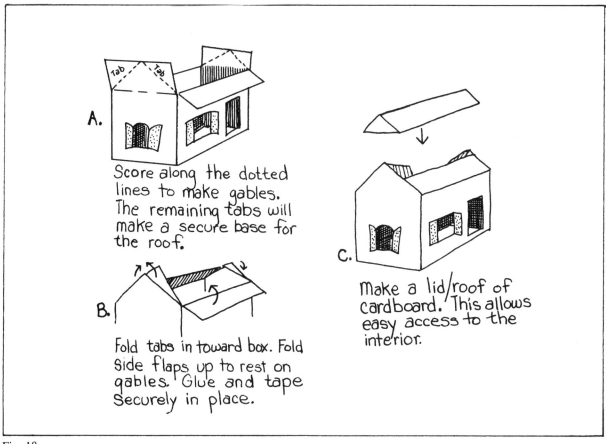

A. Score along the dotted lines to make gables. The remaining tabs will make a secure base for the roof.

B. Fold tabs in toward box. Fold side flaps up to rest on gables. Glue and tape securely in place.

C. Make a lid/roof of cardboard. This allows easy access to the interior.

Fig. 18.

First, draw in the door and windows as nearly perfectly as you can, making certain that the lines are straight to allow for easy opening and closing. It is probably best to make a pattern or template from poster paper, and trace around it onto the surface of the cardboard box. With the matt knife, score along all edges of the door, but cut through only three, leaving one on the side to provide the "hinge" (figure 19). Then score along the rectangle which will become the window. If you have decided against shutters, cut completely through each of the four lines, and remove the resulting rectangle. Shutters do lend a quaint, storybook air to the house, however, so it seems a shame not to try them out. Score along the two outer vertical lines, without cutting all the way through. These will provide the shutter hinges. To make the shutters swing outward, score along the inside of the box; to make them swing inward, score along the outside of the box. Cut completely through the two horizontal lines, and through a vertical line drawn parallel with the hinge lines, but in the exact center of the window for instant, built-in shutters.

To form a gabled roof, draw an identical triangle on each of the two small top flaps of the cardboard box, ensuring that the peak of the triangle is in the center. Score lightly along the two uppermost lines of the triangle, and bend the resulting flaps back toward the house. Use them to support the two longer pieces of the lid (which will become the roof) and to make the gable stationary. Glue them into place and secure with tape.

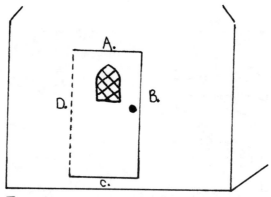

To make a door that opens,
cut out sides A, B, and C.
Score along line D on
the inside of the box
to make the door open
out; score on the outside
of line D to make the
door open in.

Fig. 19.

Depending upon the size of box, you will now have a rather long opening on the roof, big enough to insert puppets, small dollhouse furniture, and inquisitive hands. To make a removable lid-roof, which gives greater character to the house, take a piece of cardboard about one-half-inch longer than the box, making sure that there is enough to overlap both sides of the stationary panels. Score down the middle of this new roof piece lengthways and bend into position over the gables. You can then adjust the width of the cardboard roof to get the overhang right.

To make small gables for this removable roof section, draw small triangles traced from the top few inches of the stationary gables. Leave tabs or "wings" on either side of the small gables so that they may be glued to the inside of the removable roof. These small gables, which will keep the roof from slipping off, will also give greater strength and stability.

By now, the box should look very houselike. Decorating could be done by students. It is important, however, to make sure that existing windows and doors are not blocked by stray bits of construction paper, so the teacher may wish to suggest the following plan:

1. *Cover the shutters and doors.* Cut construction paper long enough to cover the shutters and doors from top to bottom with perhaps enough leeway for error. Remember that the doors and window shutters will need to be covered both front and back, so double the length required and leave a few inches to glue to the walls of the house.

Put glue onto the front of the shutter and adhere the colored paper, smoothing it free of any bubbles or wrinkles. Fold the paper over the side of the shutter. Apply glue to the back of the shutter and smooth down the paper. With the shutter closed, glue the extra construction paper along the side of the window to the box. Immediately, however, open the shutter, holding the newly glued paper in place, and work the shutter rapidly open and closed to create some elasticity across this "hinge" in colored paper.

Treat the door in exactly the same manner. Trim off excess colored paper from the top and bottom, leaving just enough to bend over the width of the shutter and door. Put glue along the top of the shutter and cover the corrugated opening with the paper. Repeat this process on the door.

Of course, you may experiment with paint, and thus avoid colored paper entirely, but all paints will cause the cardboard to warp, even if you paint both sides of the door or shutters. The colored paper laminate is the safe treatment, and also gives excellent overall coverage without brush strokes or messy cleanup.

2. *Decorate the interior of the house.* Since the Fox Box will receive little interior lighting, consider lining it with white paper to reflect any light from the outside. Decorate the interior by gluing paper (cut to fit) onto each of the four walls, leaving precisely cut openings for doors and windows. A paper carpet of a bright color will complete the interior decoration. If plain colors seem too simple, use gift-wrapping paper or fragments of wallpaper.

3. *Cover the exterior walls.* Imagination is the operative word here. Is the stucco effect desirable? Use stiff, brightly colored construction paper. Wrap it around the box, cutting window and door holes accurately where needed and glue it in place. Always place glue onto the box, not onto the construction paper. To disguise the joints where various sheets of paper will meet, cut out "ivy" from green paper or from photographs in gardening catalogs to paste over the cracks.

You may want a brick effect. A local hobby shop may sell specially printed brick paper, designed for use by model railway enthusiasts or dollhouse makers. A gift shop may even carry a stock of novelty wrapping paper with a brick motif. A very pleasant homemade brick cladding can be achieved by a group effort, however, with individually cut-to-size "bricks" glued onto the "stucco." To achieve realism, avoid using red paper only; include some brown, yellow, gray, and green occasionally, or any other colors that happen to be at hand. Making bricks of small leftover scraps helps in economizing, too.

4. *Shingle the roof.* The easy way to do this is to use plain, brightly colored construction paper, cut to fit, and glued in place. Variations could involve drawing on individual shingles, tiles, or slates. Students could cut out individual tiles or slates to glue into place, starting at the bottom of the roof and working up to the top, so that a natural overlap occurs. This is easy to do if entire rows of roofing tiles are cut out at once, using a template cut from stiff paper (figure 20).

A chimney could be added to the removable roof or to a dormer window. Modern foxes might also require a television antenna made from clothes hangers or piano wire from a model shop. Chimneys can be made from small cocoa boxes. Using the gable of the roof as a template, trace the angle onto the bottom of the cocoa box, repeating on the opposite side. Cut out the bottom of the box and the angles; the chimney should fit onto the roof perfectly.

To secure the chimney to the roof, don't cut the triangles off, but merely score along the lines with a matt knife or scissors. Cut up from the bottom center of the box to the top of the gable angle. Fold the flaps either outward or inward, apply glue to the bottoms, and stick them onto the roof, pressing down with fingers. Decorate the chimney with paper bricks or stones. The chimney should be applied to the roof before shingling.

5. *Add finishing touches.* From white or colored paper, cut and adhere door and window facings. For maximum storybook effect, go for baroque—curlicues and ribbons will enhance the architectural interest (figure 21).

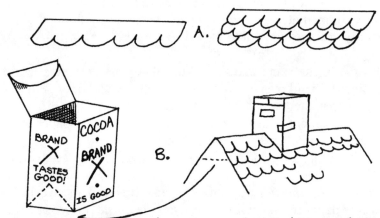

A. Tile the roof with paper strips, beginning at the bottom. Glue succeeding strips so that they overlap, like real shingles.

B. A small food box becomes a chimney. Trace the shape of the gable onto the bottom of the box, cut it out, and tape to the roof.

Fig. 20.

Fig. 21.

Glue a small flower box to the wall beneath one of the windows, preferably one that will not be liable to severe knocks in everyday wear and tear. Use an empty outer box from aspirin, perfume, or paper clips. Cover it with paper, add some paper or dried flowers, and staple and glue it to the wall.

Give the door depth by drawing in a letterbox and handle. Draw in panels or cut them from paper and glue them on. Give shutters a similar treatment or turn them into louvers by drawing in closely spaced horizontal lines.

Add a street number, or perhaps an entire street address, either directly onto the door or on a plaque glued to the side of the house. Give the house an appropriate name: Bear Lair, Dog Kennel, Cat Pad, or whatever suits the local inhabitants.

Find picture postcards of local politicians, heroes, or sports figures. Cut them out in silhouette and prop them up against the inside of the windows for a touch of fun. Or use photographs from the display in the section, "Using Photographs of Readers to Promote Reading," p. 30.

Once the house is completed, students will be able to use it in their play and in their reading. It will constantly remind them of books, especially if it has a changing stock of literature around it or on a nearby floor or table. Shy students will benefit greatly from Fox Box, for in quiet moments they may choose to take one of the inhabitants out of the house for an individual read-aloud session.

The teacher or supervisor may want to make certain rules to govern use of the box: no one may remove the puppets without first asking permission, for instance, and no roughhousing with the puppets or the box. On the other hand, the Fox Box may become an ordinary part of the surroundings, available on the same basis as any other item of equipment, even for weekend checkouts to students' homes.

Fox Box could also become Book House, used to store and display the special "Book of the Week," the "Paperback of the Day," or a selection of thematic books available for circulation. It could become Fireside Cottage, with a selection of "favorite" classics for quiet, reflective reading in the classroom or at home. Fox Box is a highly adaptable dwelling. Its charm provokes instant positive response from young readers—even from those who wouldn't dare be seen playing with dolls!

Near the Fox Box, Freddie Fox maintains a "Book of the Day" poster on a discarded easel from the art room. There is a drawing of Freddie with the legend, "Freddie Fox's Book of the Day," plus ample room on the ledge for one or two books. These books are changed every morning, and children are encouraged to take them to read. If they do decide to take them, they must escort Freddie the puppet on a short tour of the library to help him find another appropriate book of the day; thus, the display is fun, it involves searching for a good book, and it is never empty.

The puppets have also become active book promoters through their touring theatrical company, Freddie Fox's Acting Troupe, starring not only the puppets, but the children themselves. Using a collapsible cloth puppet theater, just large enough for two or three children, the puppets often tour the school to produce spontaneous plays for rapt audiences.

Capitalize upon the children's spontaneity by giving them a theme, such as "What Can I Read Next?" or "Have You Read a Good Book Lately?" and five minutes to rehearse. Two children can easily manage four puppets, one on each hand. One puppet is the bookish hero, the librarian, or the informed reader, to whom the other characters turn to find suitable, interesting books. One by one, they approach the main character, acting out their search for good books, and the hero always comes through with a good recommendation.

The audience rarely fails to enjoy the show. Often they will respond in unison to the puppets' queries. And, perhaps mercifully, the puppets never outstay their welcome on the stage; plays rarely last longer than five minutes.

MOVING BOOKS WITH MOBILES

Mobiles are used in stores of all kinds to advertise everything from soft drinks to toothpaste. Several commercial organizations also sell attractive mobiles to libraries, schools, and bookstores to promote reading, especially during Children's Book Week. But it is not necessary to part with precious funds to have highly attractive mobiles, for they are easy to make and long-lasting. Most of them also offer the added bonus of storing flat in drawers or file cabinets.

Mobiles not only move, constantly changing their appearance, but they can be made by anyone, regardless of age or lack of training. A mobile consists of various objects arranged so that they do not touch each other in their carefully balanced movements. A mobile may be highly complex, constructed of metal, glass, seashells, or wood, or it may be very simple, made totally of paper and string. A mobile may contain nothing more than ornamental objects, such as Valentine hearts or Halloween pumpkins or it may provide room for the written word. Mobiles can be used by themselves or in conjunction with larger displays. Indeed, several mobiles may be grouped together to form one basic unit.

To begin, choose the theme or message. Is there a universal symbol to represent that? Holidays abound with symbols: hearts; snowflakes; witches and their entourage of cats, brooms, and pumpkins; trees; Easter eggs. Choose one of these simple themes for the first mobile, remembering that if you can hang it, you can make a mobile out of it.

For practice, place a round dinner plate face down on a sheet of paper, ideally, paper that is colored on one side only. Trace around the plate and cut out the circle. Then draw a spiral from the outside of the circle, round and round until you reach the center. Carefully cut out the spiral. Tie a knot in the end of a string and pull the other end of the string through a hole made with a pin in the center of the spiral. For extra support, tape the knot to the bottom of the spiral.

Then hang the spiral from the ceiling, taping the string or wrapping it around a pin stuck into ceiling tiles. The spiral will fall gracefully free, rotating in the slightest current of air. Several of these spirals hung near a table of books certainly will be an eye-catcher.

To accompany a St. Valentine's Day display, start with a basic heart. Fold a piece of paper in half and draw half the heart on one side. Cut both sheets of the folded paper along the lines of the drawing until you have a Valentine heart (figure 22). Save the rest of the cutout for use in other seasonal projects.

Make several hearts in different sizes. They will become templates for the mobile. Choose the best hearts and trace around them on heavy colored paper. Red is traditional, but there is every reason to experiment with other colors. Attain added brilliance by making one half of the Valentine red, backing it with another color. As the mobile of hearts moves in the air current, the colors will shimmer beautifully. For each Valentine in the mobile, make two card Valentines. These will be glued together, with a length of cotton thread between them. Place at least two sets of Valentines, preferably of different sizes, at some point along the thread. For additional texture, make a paper lace doily to fit between all or some of the sets of hearts. To make the doily, place the heart template on ordinary white paper, and draw a wavy line all around it at least an inch larger than the original. Decorate it by piercing holes or other designs at regular intervals along the outer edge.

A simple mobile can be made by pinning or taping the threads to the ceiling, placing them far enough apart so that breezes will not entangle them. For more movement, attach two threads of hearts to both ends of a small dowel rod, available from lumber merchants and hobby shops, or for a country effect, use a twig-free branch from a tree. Piano wire or a coathanger will also work. Attach the rod, branch, wire, or coathanger to the ceiling by suspending it with thread from its center of gravity, which can be found by holding the rod lightly between the index finger and thumb at various points along the rod until it balances.

To make a more complex mobile, repeat the process with the rod (or twig, piano wire, or coathanger), attaching the smaller of the two to the end of the other. Experiment to achieve balance by sliding the suspending thread along the rod before securing it with a dab of strong glue.

The hearts can contain the titles of seasonally appropriate books, or they can speak for themselves, simply hanging over the books. Similar mobiles can enliven book displays for Christmas, Halloween, Groundhog's Day, patriotic holidays, or any other season or event. The important things to remember are (1) use appropriate colors, backing the front of each object with another color to achieve shimmering brilliance; (2) make two identical shapes for each object in the mobile; (3) make certain that the objects never touch each other in the swing—this can be done by laying the mobile out flat on a table before assembling it; (4) attach the thread so that the objects do not tilt; that is, hang the rod at the center of balance; (5) hang the mobile so that it will not touch a wall or other impediment; and (6) hang it away from severe drafts which could entangle the threads.

Using the same templates, make three hearts the same size. Or fold three sheets of paper together, so that one cut will produce three hearts. When the hearts have been cut out, staple them once or twice along the fold, having first looped the suspending thread around the fold. Open the hearts into a fan shape, and hang them from the ceiling, or use them to construct a large unit with dowel rods or piano wire. Freestanding objects can be made this way, too, provided they have a sufficient base. While hearts could not stand upon a table, Christmas trees could (see figure 23).

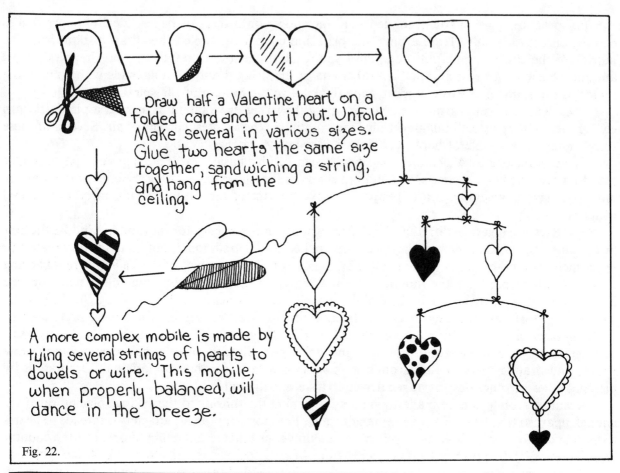

Draw half a Valentine heart on a folded card and cut it out. Unfold. Make several in various sizes. Glue two hearts the same size together, sandwiching a string, and hang from the ceiling.

A more complex mobile is made by tying several strings of hearts to dowels or wire. This mobile, when properly balanced, will dance in the breeze.

Fig. 22.

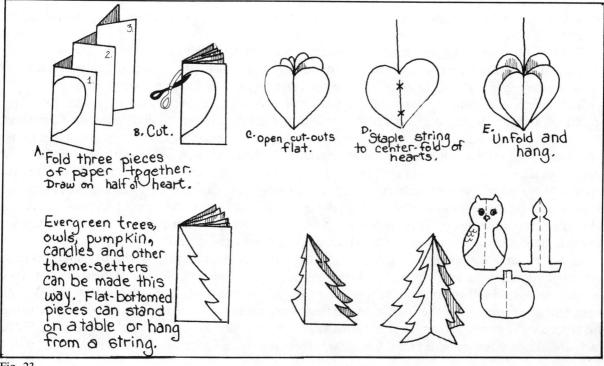

A. Fold three pieces of paper together. Draw on half of heart.

B. Cut.

C. open cut-outs flat.

D. Staple string to center-fold of hearts.

E. Unfold and hang.

Evergreen trees, owls, pumpkin, candles and other theme-setters can be made this way. Flat-bottomed pieces can stand on a table or hang from a string.

Fig. 23.

For a science fiction display, create a mobile whose parts move in several directions at once (figure 24). Cut cardboard rings in several sizes, the largest of which should not be bigger than twelve inches in diameter. Each ring should be about one-half inch in width. The diminishing rings should be an inch or two smaller in diameter than the rings immediately outside them, so that they swing freely. Attach the thread to the rings, either by the method outlined for use with double objects or connect the rings by wrapping the thread around each one once. The rings could swirl around a disk at the center or around a table-tennis ball, through which a small hole has been made to receive the end of a thread. Secure the thread with a spot of strong glue. Several concentric rings may be grouped together in one mobile or they may hang alone.

To accompany a display of books with a nautical flavor, make a mobile of sailing ships from paper, matchsticks, thread, and glue. Experiment with several kinds of boats until the right one presents itself. Flat, one-dimensional boats are just as effective as full-blown sailing ships.

A slightly more complicated masted ship requires a matchstick or cocktail stick, onto which will be fitted the sail, a square of white paper (figure 25). The hull is a flat piece of colored stiff paper, shaped like an iron, which is glued to the bottom of the mast. A larger hull could accommodate two or three masts, each having two sails. The sails may be decorated with appropriate insignia or made from colorful paper.

A variation on the ship motif includes fish, which are made from elongated teardrop shapes (figure 26). Experimentation with a pair of scissors for a few minutes will result in a school of individually shaped specimens. They may even look better if they aren't all alike. Try cutting a few from different papers, too, such as corrugated cardboard, cereal boxes, and typing paper. Punch in a hole for the eye with a paper punch if the fish is large enough or draw it in with pencil or pen.

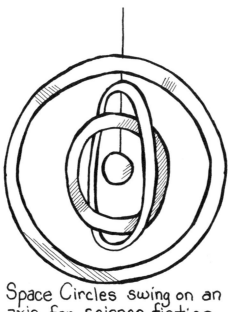

Space Circles swing on an axis for science fiction or astronomy displays.

Fig. 24.

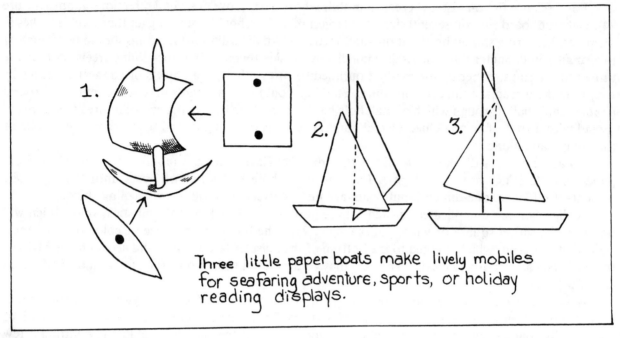

Fig. 25.

Fig. 26.

To make a more three-dimensional fish, experiment with cuts and folds. For long, flat fish, cut from the center of the tail to about the middle of the body. Cross the two parts slightly over one another and glue them in place. Cut out the mouth and paste on eyes on both sides of the body.

Achieve similar effects on the body of the round, flat fish by cutting from the edge of the circle to the exact center. Move one side of the cut slightly over the other until a little cone starts to form (see figure 27). Glue the overlap together, add eyes, and suspend. To make a fat conefish, glue two cones together, provided they are the same size. Make interesting fins by putting a long crescent shape between two cones before gluing.

Another three-dimensional sea creature can be made from folded stiff paper (figure 28). Draw the fish on one side of the folded paper, being sure to leave enough contact at the fold between the two sides of the animal so that it won't fall apart when you cut it out. Glue the mouth together after rolling the bottom pieces into an overlap. Suspend this fish by pulling a thread through the central spiny fin, securing it with a large knot and glue. Other animals may be made like this also, provided that plenty of contact is left along the fold.

Letters can be made into mobiles to suspend over general book collections for which the only theme is that of reading. It may be enough to spell out a simple word such as "READ" (figure 29) and leave it at that, but added movement and enticement comes from bookish shapes suspended from some or all of the letters. Put a different slogan on each book, perhaps to correspond with the letter from which it hangs: "Reading Is Really Rather Reviving"; "Reading Is Enjoyably Exciting"; "Reading Is Awfully Amazing"; or "Reading Is Deliciously Dandy." Using one of the stock character shapes from chapter 11, make a funny face to hang from one of the letters, making sure that each element in the face is suspended freely for movement.

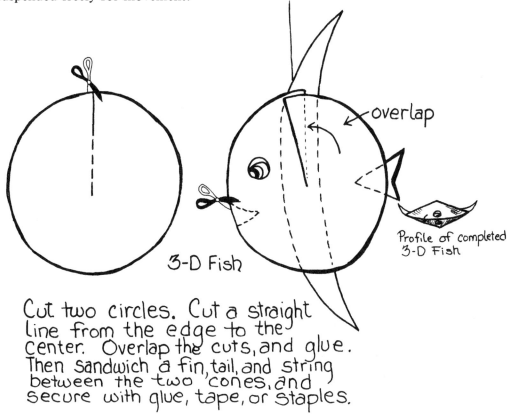

overlap

Profile of completed
3-D Fish

3-D Fish

Cut two circles. Cut a straight line from the edge to the center. Overlap the cuts, and glue. Then sandwich a fin, tail, and string between the two cones, and secure with glue, tape, or staples.

Fig. 27.

These stand-up creatures can also be suspended.

Fig. 28.

Fig. 29.

Each letter probably should be suspended from the same rod or from the ceiling so that movement will not totally reconstruct or obscure the spelling.

Colorful mobiles can be made from loops of paper. These are easily made by children, given brief instruction by an adult. It may be a good idea to start with the old-fashioned paper chain, for which you will need strips of oaktag or construction paper approximately five inches long and about one-half-inch wide. At both ends of each strip, cut a slit half the width of the paper and sloping in the same direction, making sure that the slits are cut one to a side. Curve the strip of paper back on itself and fit the slits together. Put the next strip through the first and continue until the chain is long enough, without using glue or tape. The chain has more texture than one make from strips that are glued, taped, or stapled. The advantage is that no sticky mess will have to be cleaned up afterward.

These paper chains can create a carnival atmosphere when they are draped in swags, either over one particular book display or periodically over several displays throughout the classroom, library, or other space. To hang most effectively, treat the ceiling as you would a floor on which furniture had to be arranged. Visually mark off geometric patterns, such as rectangles, squares, or circles, above the books on display and then drape the paper swags carefully, using straight pins in acoustic tiles or strong tape on nonporous surfaces. Paper chain swags can highlight auxiliary displays also, such as the card catalog, the checkout or circulation area, a storytelling area, or a speaker's platform.

To make a more defined mobile from loops, start with a theme, such as fish, birds, or trees. Using appropriately colored paper, make loops of various sizes to fill in an outer skeleton or frame of the creature in mind (figure 30). To make a fish, cut two strips of paper about twenty inches long and one inch wide. Glue the strips together at a spot about two inches from either end. Turn one end into a fishy mouth by curling the two-inch bits beyond the glue up and back to make a circle of "lips" and glue them into place. Make the tail by slightly separating the strips at the other end.

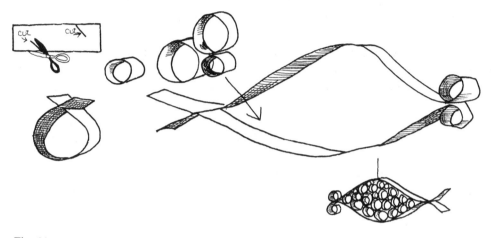

Fig. 30.

Start filling in the two strips of the framework with paper loops of different sizes. Gradually the body of the fish will expand until it can hold no more loops. Glue the loops together wherever they touch. To make an eye, place a fairly large loop near the mouth, and fill it in with progressively smaller loops, preferably of black paper. This should be the only loop with other loops in it.

To make fins, cut a strip of paper about ten inches or less long and just as wide as the body of the loop fish. Fold the short strip of paper anywhere along its length; glue both ends to the top of the fish's body, letting the middle of the fin rise slightly. Hang the mobile from the ceiling with thread strung through the paper loop nearest the top center of the body. This avoids putting too much pressure on the outer skeleton and should be quite secure.

Mobiles also can be made from small cardboard boxes of the sort used to package soap, paper clips, and rubber bands. Suspend them from the ceiling to attract potential readers to books. The addition of colored paper and string is all that is necessary. To begin, decide where a word to the wise will be sufficient, for there will not be room on a pointer box for much verbiage. Short slogans, such as "READ!" or "TRY ONE," are appropriate and will be enough to draw attention to the books beneath them. To suspend the pointer box, puncture a tiny hole in the top of the box with a needle or pin. Then insert the piece of string. To keep the box from eventually slipping off, wrap the string around a small piece of card, taping the card to the inside of the lid.

Wrap the box colorfully, just as if it were a gift. Bright plain paper will not detract from the slogan. Do not wrap up the top of the box, however, for this will form a shallow basket to hold paper flowers, stock characters, or pennants.

Tape or glue the colored paper to the box and cut out two squares of colored paper the same size as the top and bottom ends of the box. Tape the bottom piece in place (to hide the overlapping folds) and thread the string through the center of the top piece, slipping it into place. Another way to fit the top piece, avoiding interference with the string, is to cut a line from any point on the edge of the paper to the center; the string may be fed through the opening and the paper pressed onto the surface.

Fix appropriate slogans to the pointer box (figure 31) either by drawing directly onto the cover paper or by gluing plain paper plaques onto the sides of the box. The latter plan is probably better, especially if the slogans are to be changed frequently. Some slogans may be sentences of four words, one word to a side, such as "Aren't These Books Great?" or "Try One of These!" If there is not a draft of air to keep the boxes twirling, curious readers will want to read the messages, even if it means walking around the boxes.

Suspend the strings from the ceiling. Vary the level of the boxes, depending on the height of the prospective readers and the display. If they hover over a shelf or table, there may be less danger of their being damaged by an exuberant punch from a would-be prizefighter or by an inadvertent blow from the head of a stroller unaware.

These pointer boxes can serve seasonal themes with the use of appropriate colors and wording:

Halloween: Black and orange, with phrases such as "Bite into These Books!" or "Ghastly Reading for Chills!" Insert autumn leaf shapes into the basket and attach black paper bats (page 88) to the string.

Thanksgiving or *Harvest Festival:* Oranges, reds, and russets, with phrases such as "Full Baskets of Books" or "Books Bring Bountiful Blessings." Insert paper fruit shapes, wheatstalks, and leaves into the basket and attach paper leaves to the string.

Spring: Yellows and greens, with phrases such as "Spring into These Books" or "Fresh Reading for Spring." Insert spring flower and leaf shapes, rabbits, birds, or balloons into the basket. Attach birds and butterflies to the string.

Winter: Reds, greens and whites, with phrases such as "A Warm Fireside Read," "Books for Apres Ski," "Riches of Christmas Books," or "Ho! Ho! Holiday Reading!" Place real Christmas baubles in the basket. Attach cutout snowflakes or paper holly to the string.

Animals: Any appropriate color, with phrases such as "Purr-rrrr-fect Books" or "Don't Horse Around—Read!" Put paper animal silhouettes in the basket and have monkeys climbing up the string or use birds, puppies, teddy bears, or your favorite animal.

St. Valentine's Day: Red and white, with phrases such as "Books: Fall in Love!" or "Love-ly Books," with a heart to fill in the extra side.

Pointer boxes rotate in the air to spell out short messages.

Fig. 31.

Part II Display Themes

4

THE TREASURE CHEST

Nothing is more evocative than a pirate's chest. The very mention of it conjures up images of crinkled old maps, palm-fringed beaches, and a crusty sailor, ready to shout, "Ahoy, matey!" Most of all, it wakens dreams of the golden cache, wealth beyond measure, the tinkle of doubloons in your hands.

To capitalize upon that rich image and to get books to readers, build a "Pirate's Cove" somewhere in your domain. The only items necessary are a pirate, his treasure chest, and a bit of treasure. Of course, you may want to add a parrot, a palm tree, even a skull and crossbones. A secret map may come in handy, too. And speaking of secrets, this display doesn't want to shout at passersby—a nudge and a wink in a discreet corner will be enough to alert the curious.

Start with the treasure chest, which, if space is limited, may be enough on its own to entice young explorers. Do a bit of scrounging in lofts and junk shops to find an old traveling case or bedroom chest. A few dents and scratches will add to the special effect, and if it has an old-fashioned camel back, all the better. Failing the antique market or someone's attic accumulation, a perfectly passable pirate's chest can be fashioned from a packing crate, either of cardboard or wood, and while a closable lid is desirable, even that is not necessary.

A pirate chest should be rather special, so decorate it accordingly. Paint it, with skull and crossbones emblazoned prominently, or if the chest happens to be a cardboard box, cover it with sturdy colored paper, wallpaper, or burlap. Heighten the illusion of faded grandeur by lining the interior with old-fashioned printed fabric or wallpaper.

The beauty of the treasure chest, however, lies not in its decor, but in its special contents. If you wish, stock it with all sorts of adventure books, especially those with a nautical flavor. But since the object is to let young adventurers discover treasure, try filling the box with an assortment of paperbacks. Mix in picture books with novels. Add some nonfiction, too, such as the popular "how-to" books, animal care, or geography books. As far as possible, let there be something for everybody. Libraries and classrooms can use the treasure chest to display new books before they join the rest of the collection.

The treasure chest works well in odd places, such as under a table, almost out of sight or in a corner, out of the way of traffic. If the chest is discreetly positioned, then a secret map (figure 32) will not only be fun but necessary. Draw and reproduce a simple floor plan of the area, with a big "X Marks the Spot." Consider leaving part of the map blank for the children to fill in or let them "label" desks, chairs, bookshelves, and other furniture as they work their way to the treasure.

When dealing with large groups of children, allow only a few to explore the pirate's cove at one time. The space available will determine the right number. Perhaps ten young pirates could fit into the corner, but only three under the table. They will need room to maneuver, not only to shuffle among the books, but to sprawl on the floor with the ones they've chosen to examine in detail. Added fun can be had by supplying pirate hats to those visiting the cove (figure 33). These are easily made from two pieces of heavy poster paper, cut in the shape of the traditional tricorner, and glued and stapled together. Not only can the hats identify the children who are supposed to be in the cove or at the chest, they can help the adult patrol a large group to prevent overcrowding the area. Anyone not wearing a pirate hat should not be there.

Depending upon the purpose of the pirate's cove, whether merely to display books or to encourage circulation, young readers may be allowed to take treasures home. The "Head Pirate-in-Charge" may decide to check books out to readers, much as library books are circulated, or there could be a "Solemn Oath" written on "parchment" to which readers sign their names and the title of the book they take. An exchange system could enable readers to take one book for every book they bring from home, so that a constant renewal occurs. In case of the latter arrangement, the Head Pirate may need to keep a close watch on the books brought in to ensure that they are suitable.

Assuming that there is room for a graphic representation of the pirate to whom the chest belongs, either beside the treasure or elsewhere, create a dashing villain to establish the theme. Look at some old Gilbert and Sullivan scores to taste the salt and the brine. Refer to chapter 11 for the construction of stock characters, from which a suitable pirate king may emerge. Add a golden earring, appropriate naval outfit, and a sneer to the face of a basic character, and the sailor is complete. A wooden leg, a parrot, a hook where a hand should be, a Jolly Roger flying above the chest ... perhaps your own research can add a local flavor to the pirate.

An old Biblical proverb warns against hiding a lamp beneath a basket, for the light will be wasted. But there is an alluring mystery to a secret box, the contents of which are suspected to be of great beauty or value. There is also something very gratifying about children sprawled on the floor, abandoned to their books, and lost in the wanderings of their imaginations.

Combining the secret box with a huddle of children intent upon opening it is the basis of this display. Rather than placing books within easy reach, which is the more typical approach, this display, at least initially, hides books from sight, like the lamp beneath the basket—but it promises treasure to the adventurer.

CAPTAIN BOOKER HAS LOST HIS TREASURE! HELP HIS CREW FIND IT BY USING THIS **SECRET** MAP.

IF YOU FIND THE **TREASURE CHEST**, SEE WHAT'S INSIDE. TAKE A PIECE OF TREASURE **HOME!**

A treasure chest might be an old trunk, or a cardboard box.

Fig. 32.

Fig. 33.

RELATED ACTIVITIES

Hire an old film about buccaneering days, mutiny, and sailing to introduce or culminate the treasure theme. Rent a Victorian sea captain's costume from a theatrical or costume shop to dress up a mannikin.

If possible, invite an authority on sailing to speak. Or take a group of students to a marina or museum. Plan a program on life in the South Seas, with artifacts, photographs, and costumes. Write for free publicity materials from embassies, consulates, chambers of commerce, or businesses with links in areas traditionally associated with treasure lore.

5

DISPLAYS FOR HOLIDAYS

For most situations, the ideal display will combine elements of both book and nonbook systems. The two styles intermingle well, so that the same structural and design rules apply.

IDEAS FOR VALENTINE'S DAY

Using whatever space is available, this first holiday promotion combines a simple Townscape (figure 34) with bookstands, tabletops, shelves, or other horizontal surfaces to display a collection of love stories for Valentine's Day. The design is simple, with only a giant red heart relieving the severe straight lines of the bookstands and the poster paper.

Promoting teenage romantic fiction is as problematic as any topic, so it might be worth concentrating on the genre for this particular display project. Once the visual promotion becomes frilly, lusciously pink, or overly feminine, the audience dwindles. This is not a particularly sexist statement, since studies reveal that girls have much broader reading interests than do boys. To reach the larger audience, then, and to encourage boys as well as girls, who might not like the Barbara Cartland approach either, to read this type of literature, omit the chintz. Naturally, this advice may not apply in sexually segregated situations, nor is it necessary always to cater to the masses via the lowest common denominator. If, however, the title is not *too* mushy and the frills are kept low key, readers who have never tasted a love story may decide to do so, discovering a very real wealth of emotion, instead of the mawkishness they may have been led to expect. A frilly display emphasizes the stereotype that good love stories are only for girls disposed to sighing and daydreaming, not for people who want action, drama, and all the other elements of a good yarn. What a shame to cause someone to miss Julius Lester's *Two Love Stories* (New York: Dial, 1972) because the display was not quite right.

Two simple approaches to a holiday display leave out traditional Valentine frills to promote reading.

Fig. 34.

The headline is just as important as any other aspect of the Valentine display, for it must lure potential readers into what may be untrodden ground. A nonmushy headline, which avoids any stereotypical allusions to romance, is necessary. Experiment with "Reading Makes the Heart Grow Fonder," "Carried Away," or "Could It Happen to You?" You might even try "The Agony and the Ecstasy." Or try this rebus, a well-worn variation of which appears on T-shirts and bumper stickers from California to Virginia: "I ♥ a Good Book," which shifts the emphasis from one's relationship with people to books. With a title like this, those reluctant to sample romance may overcome their misgivings.

While it is generally not the purpose of this book to give specific titles to be included in thematic displays, for that will vary from place to place, a suggestion for Valentine's Day seems appropriate. If this display is to reach those who might not otherwise pick up a "romance," surprise them by including books outside that category. These titles include a romantic situation, but are not necessarily dominated by the agonies of a loving couple; some of the books are dominated, however, by agonies of another sort.

A VALENTINE BOOKLIST
Also Suitable for Bibliographic Bookmarks

Blume, Judy. *It's Not the End of the World.* New York: Bradbury Press, 1972. A young girl tries to prevent the impending divorce of her parents.

Bonham, Frank. *Gimme an H, Gimme an E, Gimme an L, Gimme a P.* New York: Scribner's, 1980. A high school boy tries to help a beautiful, suicidal girl whose emotional disturbances become increasingly evident.

Byars, Betsy. *Summer of the Swans.* New York: Viking, 1970. This book tells how a broken family, in a small mountain town, relates to mental retardation, with teenage romance skirting the periphery.

Chambers, Aidan. *Dance on My Grave.* London: Bodley Head, 1982. Does the ideal friend exist in Southend-on-Sea? Two English boys try to find out if they were meant for each other.

Elfman, Blossom. *The Girls of Huntingdon House.* Boston: Houghton Mifflin, 1972. This is a light-hearted glimpse of life in an unwed mothers' home; it is hilarious, without sermons.

Greene, Betty. *Summer of My German Soldier.* New York: Dial, 1973. This is the tale of a Nazi soldier in a POW camp in Arkansas and the girl who falls in love with him.

Horwood, William. *Duncton Wood.* London: Hamlyn, 1980. This is an allegorical animal fantasy in which love, romantic and platonic, eventually triumphs over evil in a mole colony.

Konigsburg, E.L. *Journey to an 800 Number.* New York: Atheneum, 1982. Max goes to stay with his father when his mother remarries and goes on her honeymoon. Max learns something about himself—and about camels!

Strasser, Todd. *Rock 'n' Roll Nights.* New York: Delacorte, 1982. Unable to book any decent gigs for his band, Gary dreams of becoming a rock star and having a girlfriend.

Yep, Laurence. *Kind Hearts and Gentle Monsters.* New York: Harper & Row, 1982. Logical Charlie, an excellent student, meets illogical Chris, who thinks with her feelings, and their friendship surprises them both, especially since it began with hatred.

Zindel, Paul. *My Darling, My Hamburger.* New York: Harper & Row, 1969. Set in an American high school during senior year, a girl finally gives her boyfriend what he wants, with tragic consequences.

The Valentine design can be converted into any theme by substituting another symbol for the heart: a snowflake for winter or Christmas; a pumpkin for Thanksgiving, Harvest Festival, or Halloween; a giant leaf for autumn; an animal silhouette for conservation or animal fantasy.

Colors are important: a light background can brighten up a dark room; black can emphasize a dark corner, making the display capitalize upon the lack of light. Because this is such an easily convertible display, it may be wise to use a fairly neutral background color at the beginning; that is, a color that will lend itself to different themes, so that once the display is made, it can remain in use for some weeks, highlighting a different literary theme with minimal changes. A white background is ideal, but the supply of materials in the storage cupboard may largely determine color choice.

CHRISTMAS DISPLAYS

Even in our secular, multiethnic, and religiously polarized society, few people can object to a jolly Santa Claus in a public display area. He has, after all, transcended his once-saintly image in the popular imagination, evolving into gnome, dwarf, and managing director of an international firm specializing in Yuletide benefaction to faithful and nonfaithful alike. He visits some countries on a white horse, others in a sleigh pulled by reindeer, yet others in helicopters and rockets. This particular Santa (figure 35) is part twentieth-century advertising and part Victorian schmaltz, a Christmas card memorial to earliest childhood memories. But to simplify things, he's left his reindeer outside long enough to pose for a solo portrait, easily made from the basic seasonal colors of red and green.

The title is an obvious pun on the ubiquitous Christmas salutation. Other alternatives are "Santa's Reading List" or "A Book in Your Stocking," but they lack the excitement of a verb, and probably observers will have a chuckle over the original. They may even prefer "Put some Ho-ho-ho in your Holiday Reading!"

Use your own individual preference for the background, the first piece of any display to go up. A light blue is suitable, and might be enhanced by placing a curving hill of white snow beneath it, perhaps with the outline of a snow-laden forest or of a cottage on the crest to the right of Santa (figure 36). Another possibility is the *Georgian Shop Window:* make a white windowframe of strips of paper and place them over a black background. Add interest by placing simulated toys and Christmas presents on the window shelf, all made one-dimensionally of wrapping paper, ribbon, and construction paper (see figure 36). Put some snow in the corners of the panes, as if collected there during a snowfall. Snow can be very realistic if torn from white paper so that the top edges are softly frayed.

The *Dickensian Townscape* (figure 37) is a third idea for the Christmas background. Keep it simple by silhouetting the buildings in dark gray or black, highlighted by one or two yellow window shapes here and there. If the silhouette is gray, make the sky black, with a white moon and a few small stars or with the traditional Christmas star. These three ideas work well enough without overlaying the Santa figure.

To ornament the Santa figure, however, the easiest background of all is the *Solid Plane,* made from one basic color, with not a single star, bauble, or rooftop to mar the surface. Rich greens make good Christmas backgrounds, especially if they are flocked in pseudovelvet elegance. Fabric is easy to use this way also, and the textural difference highlights the paper Santa.

No matter what background is used, the display is framed in green holly leaves with red and white berries. To avoid the chore of cutting out each individual specimen, try these tricks: (1) place three or four sheets of paper together and staple them in several places along the outside edges so they don't slip about as you cut (figure 38); draw the holly leaf or leaf cluster on the top sheet and cut through all four sheets with heavy scissors; (2) cut a long strip of green, as long as the length or width of the display if possible, and about five inches wide. Cut along each edge, making holly leaf shapes as you go, preferably without drawing them in with pencil first, for this makes the process unnecessarily tedious at worst and lengthy at best. Just make the leaves uneven, as in nature. At intervals, place some of the

Fig. 35.

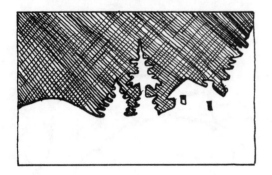 

Fig. 36.

Fig. 37.

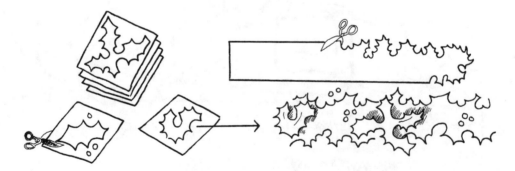

Fig. 38.

individually cut clusters to create shadows, texture, and realism. Curl the individual pieces by folding them lightly around a pencil to achieve the effect of spiked holly leaves (see figure 39).

Finish the border, which can be made of several shades of green to emulate real holly, with berries snipped from leftover scraps of red and white paper. These can be made in clusters, too. Put the berries in bunches all around the holly border. Attach them with glue so that they cover up some of the staples holding the backing sheet onto the display wall.

Put the holly leaves to work in other seasonal ways, such as the traditional Christmas wreath (figure 40). Using the top or bottom of a round wastebasket as a template, trace a circle on a sheet of green paper. Then draw leaf shapes irregularly around this, inside and out or, if you are confident

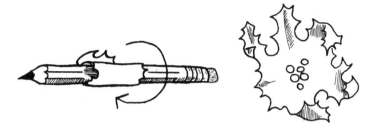

Fig. 39.

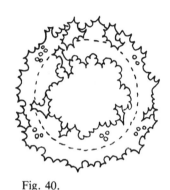

Fig. 40.

enough, go straight for the scissors, cutting without the initial drawing. But if you do draw in the leaves first, turn the wreath over onto the reverse when you have finished to hide the pencil marks.

Further enhance the wreath with a cutout red ribbon which should be glued to the bottom center (figure 41). The best shape is rather like that of a butterfly in a frock coat. If you choose, cut out a white candle to glue behind the wreath. Make it more realistic by including shapes of melting wax in the silhouette. Add a yellow-orange flame if you are prepared to tell youngsters why the flame won't ignite the holly! Complete the wreath with a few bunches of berries and some individually cut and curled leaves for texture.

If you'd rather not put in a candle, experiment with other wreath-fillers, such as white doves, fruit shapes, Christmas baubles cut from foil paper, peppermint candy canes, or wrapped presents. These wreaths can be placed at intervals around your book space—on shelf ends, windows, desks, or as mobiles. If you decide to make mobiles (figure 42), however, glue or staple two wreaths together before hanging them since single ones could flop into unrecognizable shapes after a few hours in midair. Double-sided wreaths also hide the fact that the candle is merely glued onto the back.

For Santa himself, you need bright red for his suit and hat; white for his hair, beard, fur trim, and gloves; and salmon pink for his chubby face, plus some black for his belt. Kitchen foil or other metallic paper makes a very suitable belt buckle. If you wish, convert the admittedly American Santa Claus into Father Christmas or Saint Nicholas. To Anglicize him, do away with the hat. Father Christmas wears a hooded cape, probably left over from his more saintly days when he tramped about Europe rescuing sailors and children. Nothing could be easier than this change of habit, but be sure to add some white hair beneath the hood (figure 43).

To dress him as Saint Nicholas takes a bit more research, especially if you plan to follow the Dutch custom closely, but he looks just as jolly in ecclesiastical gear as in his snowsuits. His hat (figure 44) becomes a miter, with or without the cross, and his colorful outfit transforms into a bishop's cope,

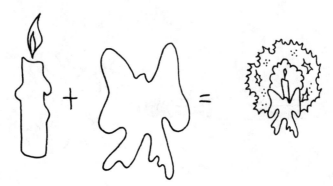

Fig. 41.

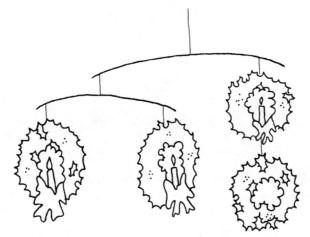

Fig. 42.

In England, Santa Claus is called Father Christmas. He wears a hooded cape that reaches to his boots.

Fig. 43.

Santa Claus dons full ecclesiasticals to visit Austria and the Low Countries.

Fig. 44.

beneath which is a white surplice. Easy enough, really, and an illustration of a Christmas tradition in the Low Countries or Germany where gifts are given on December 6, Saint Nicholas's feast day. If you do choose in favor of the Saint, be certain to provide some backup reading material about Saint Nicholas. This information could come in the form of a bookmark, a mimeographed Christmas card, or a simple fact sheet, including, of course, the sponsoring organization's address and phone number, opening hours, and other pertinent information.

To encourage younger readers' participation in the display, put a mailbox nearby, appropriately colored and decorated, into which they may drop their letters to Santa (figure 45). (You, of course, must ensure that they actually reach Santa by the cutoff dates: December 5 in Holland; December 24 in England and America!) Cover a cardboard box with red paper, put a slit in one side, give it the label customary in your area (mailbox, post box, letterbox), and the postal system is ready. A poster nearby will help to explain the mechanics involved (figure 46). You might even sell charity stamps at a nominal fee, giving proceeds to the organization who supplied them. Or have the letter-senders design their own stamps, then donate a small sum toward a specific charity when they post their letters in your box.

A variation on the letter-writing theme takes the form of a mini book review. Instead of sending St. Nick a list of desirable consumer goods, youngsters tell him about one of the books they've read which he, too, will like. It could be a Christmas book, a winter's tale, or any book. In this special letter, they explain why he will like the book as much as they did. Santa may choose to exhibit the best letters nearby, and if he has the time, could even pen a short reply! He might even manage to give a prize to the writer of the most original letter.

To distribute a list of suggested seasonal readings, incorporate them into the display by placing them in a pouch in Santa's hand (figure 47). Make the reading lists large enough and the pouch small enough so that the bibliographies don't get lost inside. If the lists are small enough to slip out of sight, eager readers will inadvertently tear the pouch off the wall. The bibliographies may take the form of a letter from Father Christmas, addressed to his *Dear Readers.*

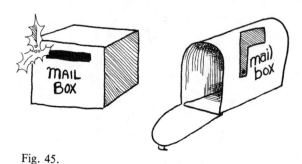

Fig. 45.

Fig. 46.

Make the pouch from two heavy pieces of paper, preferably green or red. Cut out the back sheet first, then the front, making this one larger in order to fold the sides around the back, paper doll fashion, and to form the actual body of the pouch on the wall.

Another participatory device is the *Santa Claus Trail,* with prizes or recognition for those who follow it. The Trail consists of sets of questions and/or problems which participants must answer by a specified time or date in order to win the prize, which might be a chocolate chip cookie, a handful of popcorn, or an ornament from the library Christmas tree. Ideally, the book displayer will put up a new set of problems at least every other day, so that by the end of the time period, the participants will have answered between ten and twenty questions. The questions can cover any seasonal topic, but for book displays, they should center on holiday books. Questions can range from names of authors, titles of books, and lines of poems to more detailed ones about styles of illustration, dates, or plots.

Various levels of difficulty can cater to a wide age range with separate trails for children, young adults, and older readers, depending upon the local constituency. Middle school classrooms or libraries could use the Santa Trail as a special learning exercise in teaching students the use of reference materials, indexes, tables of contents, and intuitive reasoning. The questions should not be too difficult, for the purpose of the Trail is to attract readers to the books. The insertion of local-color questions, unrelated to books or the display, is certainly permissible, for youngsters enjoy finding out

Fig. 47.

the name of Miss Webster's Yorkshire terrier or the number of guppies in Mr. Bergstrom's fishtank; these questions make the game interesting, varied, and surprising.

To attract participants initially, put the problems or questions behind one-dimensional Christmas presents on the display board (figure 48). By lifting the present, the participant reveals the set of questions. Every other day, the displayer will add another present to the display, with its set of problems. At the end of the event or promotion, the participants will have worked their way through several books in search of correct answers! Accommodate latecomers to the scheme by posting all the problems to date beneath an especially large present on the display. As new sets of questions are added, be sure to add them to the cumulative list.

Small gifts, such as pencils, writing pads, or bookmarks make good awards to those who complete the Trail. Adults will enjoy the competition if they know that some winners—the first three to complete, perhaps—will receive a bottle of wine. Or every person who enters could receive a lottery ticket, the grand prize being a bottle of champagne.

These ideas can become Halloween promoters through clever adaptations: Santa becomes a warlock or a witch or a benevolent wizard. The Dickensian Townscape remains the same, but a few small jack-o-lanterns might be added to decorate the window openings. The border of holly could be autumn leaves, instead, made in the same method. The pouch becomes a trick-or-treat bag. Readers could follow the *Pumpkin Trail*.

Make these gifts by folding a piece of colored paper in half. Cut a ribbon from a complimentary color and glue it to the top of the present. Write a Santa Trail question inside.

Fig. 48.

For Easter or spring, Santa becomes a fat bunny. The background of blue with snow becomes a spring sky with a green meadow. The border, too, reflects the season with daffodils and green leaves. Instead of a Santa Trail, readers could hop along the *Bunny Trail*.

Other festivals and seasons can be celebrated through similar book displays, all of which may be easily adapted from the basic ideas presented here. The process remains the same, but the results will reflect unique seasonal requirements.

A TABLE CENTERPIECE

As a table centerpiece at Christmas, this tree will add seasonal gaiety while promoting holiday reading. The only special tool needed is a matt knife to cut the cardboard box, which will then be covered with green paper and put to the task of displaying books (figure 49). It may be necessary to have two fairly large cardboard boxes, such as those in which a television is packed, although a substantial tree can be made from only one box. To begin, draw a line diagonally from one corner of the box to another, creating two triangles. Label one corner A and the opposite corner B. Return to corner A and down the other side of the box, draw another diagonal line to corner C. Using the matt knife, carefully cut along the lines. Draw a semicircular shape on the "floor" or base of the box between points B and C. Cut this out with the knife.

Turn the box over and repeat this process on the remaining sides. When you have cut as many of these open pyramids as possible (usually two from one large box), set aside the scraps, and draw in stylized evergreen shapes down one side of the pyramid (figure 50). Use the first evergreen tree shape as the template for all the others so that they are identical. Cut a small short slit near the end of each bough, except the bottom ones, which will later hold a cardboard garland.

Put the pyramids back-to-back on a table to see how the tree is shaping up. At this point, you may decide that you need to make another pyramid from the extra box or you may be happy with the two or three from the first one. Essentially, the tree is composed of four quarters. Looking at it from above (figure 51), it is easy to see that several arrangements of the tree segments are possible, including one which uses only two pyramids.

Select a rich green paper, large enough to cover each of the sides of the tree, front and back. Use the stylized tree shapes as a template to cut the green paper covers and cut out enough to enclose the

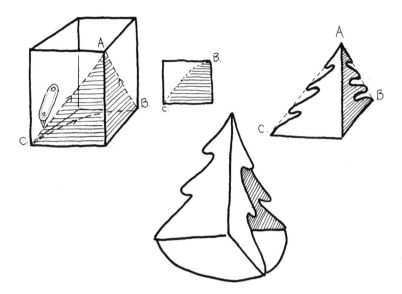

Fig. 49.

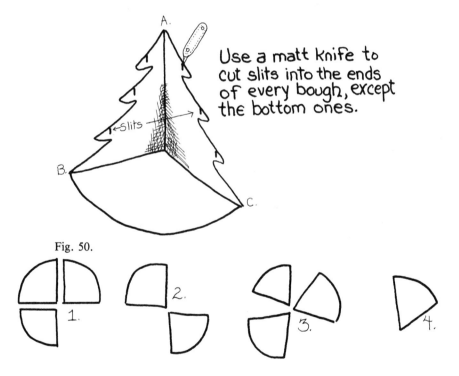

Use a matt knife to cut slits into the ends of every bough, except the bottom ones.

←Slits

Fig. 50.

These trees may be arranged in different patterns, singly or in groups, as shown by this top view of four different clusters.

Fig. 51.

tree completely. You will need to make the paper laminate slightly larger than the cardboard in order to overlap the width of the corrugated box.

Glue the green paper onto the cardboard. Then cut a red "carpet" to cover the circular floor at the base of the tree or use Christmas gift-wrapping paper for added interest. The tree is almost ready to receive its ornamentation of books, but first put the slits to use. From the scraps of cardboard left over from the pyramids, fashion connecting strips (figure 52) long enough to overreach the distance between the sides of the tree. Cut a slit at each end of the connecting garland at the point at which it will join the slit in the tree. Cover the strips with green paper or other appropriately colored material, and fit the strips into place.

Add a few seasonally decorated pointer boxes (see page 45) with appropriate slogans: "Great Reading for Christmas," "Jolly Books, Jolly Season," "The Night before Christmas," or "Books Make Good Gifts." Suspend the boxes at different heights and intersperse them with a few more stars to create a fairyland effect.

A forest of small trees can join the main cardboard tree (figure 53). Again, as in the star method, fold up to five pieces of green paper together. On one side, starting at the top of the fold, draw half an evergreen tree shape in a diagonal to the bottom of the sheet of paper. Cut it out, staple together along the fold, and open the pieces out like a fan to make freestanding stylized trees. These trees can stand on flat surfaces, alone or in groves, or they may be suspended by strings from the ceiling. Children enjoy making these trees, which can be used as inexpensive Christmas cards, as bookmarks, or as decorations to take home—the free gift from the display to the reader.

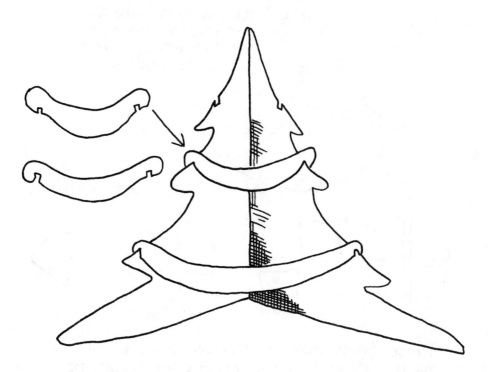

Fig. 52.

Fig. 53.

These trees can be used without the Christmas flourishes to support a display about ecology and natural resources. Instead of baubles and stars, use teddy bears and stuffed toys. Display books on conservation, animals, geology, and natural history. The trees help create a country atmosphere, too, for local patriotic displays on Davy Crockett, Mike Fink, or Paul Bunyan; state centennials; regional homecomings; or arts and craft displays.

Put the tree on a table, add a few traditional ornaments—glass baubles, garlands, and reindeer—and place seasonal books all around the base. Some books may stand upright, the boards open to support them, while others may lean against the tree, and still others may lie on their sides. Intersperse a few ornaments among the books on the tabletop to make the scene more festive.

Suspend a star from the ceiling to hang just above the top of the tree. A multidimensional star is easily made by cutting two or more identical shapes and stapling them together along the fold (figure 54). First, fold together between two and five stiff pieces of paper eight inches square until they are exactly eight by four inches. Draw half a star shape on one side and cut it out slowly so that the scissors will penetrate the several sheets of paper evenly. Open the cutout stars, staple in the center, and suspend from the ceiling with cotton thread. Suspend singly or in clusters over the pyramidal tree.

Since this cardboard tree is in segments, it does not have to be used solely as a table centerpiece. Half of the tree could be used against a wall. Quarter sections of the tree can be stood in a corner or used alone on a shelf or table.

To dismantle and save, remove the cross-pieces and put them in a large envelope. The segments can be nestled into each other and put out of the way in a storage cabinet or closet. If storage space is a great problem, use the matt knife to cut the base of the tree from one of the sides so that the entire piece can be folded flat, using the remaining connection as a hinge. Or if storage is absolutely minimal for something this size, make a neighboring classroom or library happy by giving your used display materials to them, perhaps in exchange for something of theirs which you can use.

Fig. 54.

RELATED IDEAS

For Easter, instead of a tree, make a basket. Cut a large cardboard box roughly in two, leaving perhaps two-thirds of it intact. Around this frame, build up an ornamental layer of woven paper basketry, either in earth tones or in brilliant spring colors. Make a handle from bits of the discarded cardboard, fill the basket with straw or shredded paper, and then add books.

Make a tabletop sign that says, "Look What the Easter Bunny Brought!" And he need not bring just books about Easter. Attractive Easter eggs are available commercially, or an activity group could be organized to make their own, in conjunction with the seasonal book display. A stuffed toy rabbit would not be amiss, either, or a cartoon one could be made using the stock character collage method (see chapter 11).

For Halloween, create a tombstone from a large cardboard box. Turn the box onto its bottom so that it stands tall vertically. Cover it in white or gray paper, and with a black felt-tip pen, add an inscription: "Here Lies GHASTLY READING—May It *Not* R.I.P." Ghost stories and other seasonal titles could lie about the base of this tombstone, which could be secured to the display surface with tape or by weighting it internally with a heavy object.

Create additional fun for browsers by making a sarcophagus from two boxes, one for the upright stone and the other to be placed horizontally in front of it, with a spooky top that can be opened by interested viewers! For extra fun, make a creepy vampire hand emerging from the lid of the horizontal tomb by stuffing a glove with tissue and attaching it to a stuffed outfit inside the box, complete with Halloween mask. Store the books beside the vampire.

6

SAILING AND
THE SEA

Was it an advertising billboard for suntan oil that inspired this display or was it a travel agent's poster about Cyprus? The image was so vivid that it remains long after the product or destination vanished from memory and the design is perfect for a general display of books on a loosely related theme.

In the original advertising artwork, vivid oranges, reds, and yellows swam over and into each other to create a feeling of Mediterranean heat. A large red setting sun was visible behind the stylized clouds. And it was all so very simple!

This display can promote a summer reading program, even when there is no specific theme. The books can be made available near the wall display, which speaks for itself in eloquent dignity. "Summertime and the Readin' Is Easy" recalls the Gershwin tune, but any other title would do: "A Warm Day, a Cold Drink, and a Good Book," "Perfect Weather for Reading," or "Thirsty? Drink Up a Good Book."

If your classroom, library, bookshop, or other display space has a vast, empty wall, the summertime display will be just as eye-catching as the original billboard which inspired it. The larger the space, the better, especially if it can be viewed from far across the room or building. The idea can, of course, be pared down to fit onto an existing bulletin board.

To achieve a summer heat wave of reading (figure 55), alternate hazy clouds in bright yellows and oranges. Fire-engine red can make the sun and the lettering blaze on this display to fill a wall or it can be reduced to fit a picture frame.

A similar idea is to create a tropical sunset of concentric circles, using sky colors of fire reds and bright yellows, the reflections of blues and greens, and mirror images, highlighted with a palm tree. Add a sailing ship in the water or a bird circling lazily in the sky.

For further detail, add the silhouette of a reader, sitting with his back to a shady tree, book in hand. The silhouette should be just that, with no detail at all. The character could be of a color complementary to the overall scheme or of traditional black. Use an opaque projector to enlarge a photograph of a fisherman from a sports magazine, a swimmer lounging by a pool, or any other appropriate person. Failing those means, "hire" a friend or a student to sit behind a powerful light so

Fig. 55.

that his or her shadow is cast onto a blank wall, over which you have taped several contiguous sheets of plain paper. Trace the shadow for a very personalized reader's silhouette.

This idea can be converted for use in winter by changing the colors to shades of blue and white. A heading such as "Wintertime: A Warm Hearth and a Good Book" may suffice to attract readers to your carefully selected collection. The addition of a snowscape with stylized evergreen trees and a country cottage will not detract from the effect. When seasonably appropriate, a certain jolly elf with his team of reindeer could course through the sky or across the snow below.

For use in spring, or when a temperate summer is in view, modify the stylized clouds with blues and whites, but in warmer tones than those used in the winter scene. The sun may be golden, though in winter it should be white or the very palest yellow. In spring, a green landscape, kept in simple silhouette, may enhance the display.

A large wall attraction, such as this, does not need a special collection of books near it, though you may wish to add some. This type of display may be just the decorative statement you need to call attention to the entire library or bookshop and to implant the idea in passersby that "Yes, I must drop by and pick up a good book for the weekend."

The sea could be hundreds of miles away without dampening the spirits of the crew aboard this frigate (figure 56), which sails happily across vast expanses of corridor, classroom, or library. Make her large and dignified to attract readers' attention from far away or make her petite and cheeky for a small tabletop tableau. She can be highly detailed, with timbers, portholes, and sophisticated nautical mechanisms, or simple and plain, dependent upon form alone to lift the imagination away from the classroom and out to sea with a good book. She embodies the spirit of adventure, however large or small she is, and the nautical display around her will transform any room into the bounding main.

While this display could be used with a study of the sea and seamanship, it is so adaptable that many other uses will be found. Build the display to promote historical fiction, adventure, or a collection of books especially for the summer holidays, or turn it into a travel agency to promote literature set in foreign lands.

Headlines and titles will turn up in abundance: "Put the Wind in *Your* Sails with These Good Books," "Hoist Up a Good Book," "Sail Away with a Good Book," or if the whiskey people wouldn't mind, "Afore Ye Go ...." Let the title reflect the intention of your display so that passersby will taste the flavor immediately and want to devour more: "Ahoy, Mates!" Small subheadings will creep up in unlikely places, providing humor and encouragement. The fish could say, "Hello, sailor!" The octopus could ask, "Could you direct me to Davey Jones's locker?" The crew could shout "Ahoy, readers!" The vessel herself could be christened *H.M.S. Readalot* or *U.S.S. Literature*. And don't forget to put titles on the books the characters are reading!

Before initial enthusiasm is blown away by the monsoon of doubt, let it be emphasized that the display need not be difficult to put together. Complicated, yes; and fairly involved, yes; but difficult, not necessarily! A detailed examination of the components should reassure the fainthearted, so with scissors at the ready and compass in hand, do not hesitate to embark.

The sea is very easily made from rolls of paper, cut in a wave pattern, one role lapping over the other until the desired depth is reached (figure 57). Usually, three tiers of water will do. Make them from seagreen, aquamarine, dull battleship gray, or other ocean-like colors. If rolls are not available, ordinary sheets of paper will suffice. The important thing is to make each wave exactly like the other, for this sea should be very stylized. If the waves are all different, the effect will not be that of a whimsical, sophisticated display. Practice making one good wave until it is good enough to become the template for all the others. Study the works of Japanese painter and woodcut artist Hokusai

Fig. 56.

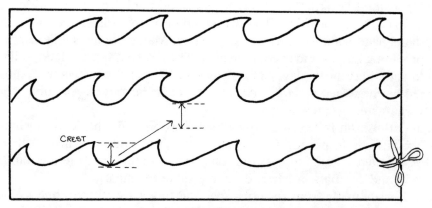

Economize on paper consumption: cut as many layers of waves per sheet as possible. This will be determined by the height of the crest of the wave. Allow enough space between that and the next line of waves so that gaps will not show when they are mounted on display, tile- or clapboard-style.

Fig. 57.

(1760-1849) to see fine examples of stylized wave patterns suitable for modification in a display such as this.*

While the sea is in construction, think of some friendly creatures to place between the waves (figure 58): a fish or two, certainly, and an octopus; a mermaid, a whale, a sea serpent; perhaps a Nessie-like monster, or dolphins and seagulls. If the wallspace is truly large, then a vast community of inhabitants could live happily together, all made from stock characters (see chapter 11). But do avoid clutter. Just as the classroom aquarium can support only so many fish before overpopulation causes problems, this sea of paper must wave about unhindered by too many scaly beings.

Depending upon the original wall covering at hand, it may not be essential to provide a background sky. A plain wall could provide a pleasant horizon, but feel free to put up a blue background, perhaps with clouds, similar to that used in the "Summertime" display on page 70, or any other sky effect deemed appropriate.

Having survived thus far, you arrive at the most complicated bit of engineering in the display, the stately sailing ship. Since she is a three-dimensional vessel, with sails literally billowing in imaginary gusts, think in terms of bulges and bas-relief, created from stiff paper with strategic cuts and positioning on the wall.

The hull of the ship could be made from a large cardboard container such as those used to package refrigerators. It also could be made just as well from two or three stiff pieces of construction paper, stapled and glued together (figure 59). Draw in the outline of the hull lightly, using an opaque projector, if necessary, to reproduce a smaller drawing or photograph of an actual ship. Stylize the drawing, though, so that the shape remains simple, easy to cut out and assemble.

Cut the sails from white, off-white, or light tan construction paper. Heavy cardboard boxes are too thick to make effective sails, which need to bend without creasing when they reach the display wall. Add depth to the display by making the sails diminish into the distance slightly. This simple trick of perspective can be achieved by drawing a long triangle lightly on the paper, then joining the top and bottom lines by parallel curves.

The masts are long pieces of paper, black or dark brown, which taper slightly toward the top. A crow's nest graces the central mast. This is little more than a round box, from which a sailor can lean perilously, book in hand. Use heavy twine or light brown yarn to create an interesting set of ropes that can be stapled or glued to the wall. Fly a banner or flag from the top mast or from the rigging at the rear and H.M.S. Readalot is practically afloat.

Putting her on the wall presents a few problems, none of which, however, will sink the project. In order to create the three-dimensional bas-relief, lightly pinch the forward end of the hull toward the rear. The middle of the ship will bulge outward automatically. The sails, too, can billow by lightly bending or pinching the tops toward the bottoms. Practice folding them on the work surface before attempting to put them on the wall.

The first item to go up should be the hull of the ship. To give the impression of a rigger in full flight, set her at a slight angle—not too much, lest her crew be in danger! To create a mood of quiet sailing in a calm wind with time aplenty for readings, set her perfectly horizontal. Staple, glue, or otherwise affix one end of the hull to the wall, remembering then to pinch the other end toward the middle to get the bulge. Fix the hull in place all along the ends and bottom, but not along the top, which must remain fat and open, not only to receive the bottoms of the masts, but to look right.

*See the following books for further information on Hokusai: Jack Hillier, *Art of Hokusai in Book Illustration* (Sotheby Parke Bernet, 1980); Jack Hillier, *Hokusai: Painting, Drawings, and Woodcuts* (Phaidon, 1978); James A. Michener, ed., *Hokusai Sketchbooks: Selections from the Manga* (Charles E. Tuttle, 1958); E. F. Strange, *Hokusai, the Old Man Mad with Painting* (Folcroft Library Editions, 1977); and Michael Sullivan, *Chinese and Japanese Art* (Grolier, 1965).

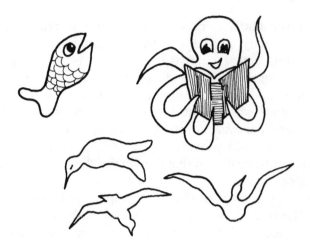

Fig. 58.

The next items to go up are the masts. They should be long enough to disappear completely into the hull. Next attach the rope rigging. It is not necessary to tie short horizontal strings to the long verticals, though that may achieve greater realism. It is simple enough to fix the top of the ropes to the central mast, fan them out toward the bottom, where they are similarly taped or stapled. The horizontals can be glued or stapled in place in situ.

You may add the crow's nest now or wait until the sails have been put in place. Put the rear sail up first and move toward the front so that the forward sails can overlap. Four tacks, pins, or staples, one in each corner, should be enough to keep the sails in fine billow. The corners of the forward sails which overlap and rest upon the sails immediately behind them should be taped, stapled, or glued to the preceding sail, and not fixed through the sail onto the wall, for that would destroy the carefully achieved billow.

While putting up the sea, think of the crew: a haughty captain, with a sword and tall hat; sailors lounging among the rigging; a first mate waving from the crow's nest—or pirates! Skull and crossbones! Booty! But pay enough attention to the first set of waves to ensure that they are perfectly horizontal. The top crest of waves goes up first and should cover the bottom of the hull. The middle crest follows and then the other. Insert the sea creatures here and there, but preferably toward the center of the display, around the ship, to concentrate attention there. Avoid a sea creature whose eyes lead away from the center of the display; make the fishes point toward the ship. Dolphins should leap forward in the same direction as the ship, leading the eye onward.

If it seems unkind to include the flat-earth joke in the display, whereby the regal ship is bound for the falling-off point, end the sea waves at a convenient margin, either with a paper border, or at the end of the wall.

Populate the ship with the friendly crew of readers. Cut their garments from old bits of cloth or wrapping paper or color them with felt-tip pens or poster paints. Follow the collage method to create stylized sailors to avoid overcomplication. Keep facial features simple; huge smiles and dots for eyes will do. And include female crew!

Make natty head gear, such as stovepipe hats, kerchiefs, and cloth caps, from bits of paper or fabric remnants. Draw on a few tattoos. Pierce an ear or two. Add a pirate or a monkey. Draw a stack of books to place in the "hold," but visible beneath the central mast.

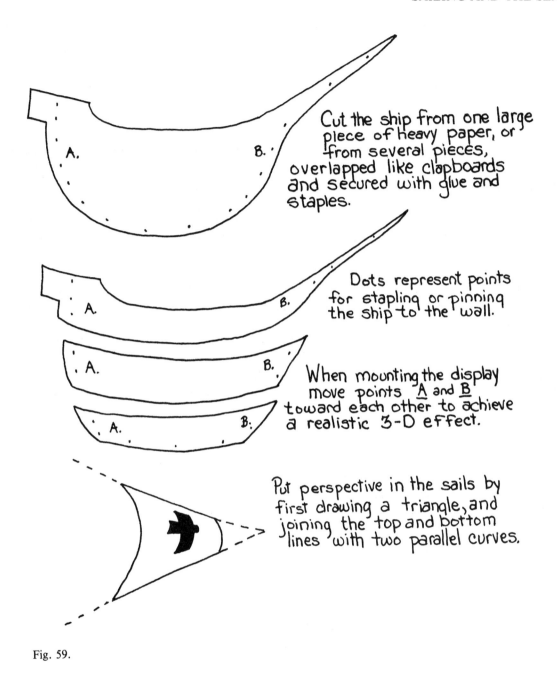

Cut the ship from one large piece of heavy paper, or from several pieces, overlapped like clapboards and secured with glue and staples.

Dots represent points for stapling or pinning the ship to the wall.

When mounting the display move points A and B toward each other to achieve a realistic 3-D effect.

Put perspective in the sails by first drawing a triangle, and joining the top and bottom lines with two parallel curves.

Fig. 59.

The project is almost finished, lacking only the title and the books for the display. While cutting out the letters for the headline, think of how the books fit into the picture. Is there a real dinghy handy, resting in the back garden, that could be brought into the room awhile? Put it beneath the display and fill it with books. Is there a low table or are some shelves available? Should books be placed on the floor beneath the paper sea? Could you recycle the pirate's treasure chest (page 49)?

Is there a bibliography to accompany the display, perhaps in the form of bookmarks or brochures, listing the books under promotion? Could a small paper dinghy or floating barrel be added to the seascape to serve as a pouch for the handouts? Is there a cardboard box or an old Victorian storage chest available that could be placed in "Davy Jones's Locker" beneath the waves to hold the books?

Younger readers will enjoy making captain's hats to wear while they are browsing among the books. If it is not convenient or if space does not allow the children to make their own, the book promoter can make a supply of hats for readers to wear while they are enjoying the books (figure 60). A variation on the basic design of the tricorner will give you a set of tea-cozy-shaped nautical hats. Cut out two templates, vaguely semicircular but slightly top-heavy, and use to make hats from blue, black, or other appropriate paper. Staple and glue them together along the top of the circles and the hat is ready. Adornments could include feathers, jewels, medals, or badges, all made from paper. Badges might say "Captain Read," "Brigadier Readalot," "First Mate Fiction Fancier," or "Pirate Browsabout."

When the tall ship has served its purpose or has been up long enough to cause visual fatigue, carefully take it down, preserving all the pieces in a safe storage place. Leave the waves, however, for the bounding main is about to become a quiet upcountry river. Remove the octopuses then, and all the other creatures, to make way for a trout, a frog, and a bankside rat or badger. A friendly dinghy is about to sail downstream, a reader in the bow, and instead of "Sailing Away with a Good Book," this display will proclaim "Lazy Days Are for Reading!"

Insert a riverbank behind the waves, with some tall grass and rushes, and the original display has doubled its lifetime, saving the book promoter the effort of making an entirely new device. The river setting can promote well-loved classics, borrowing ideas, in fact, from Kenneth Grahame's *Wind in the Willows* (New York: Penguin, 1984) or it can push more holiday reading, books about the countryside, or animal fantasies (figure 61).

Instead of a boy or girl in the boat, put an animal at the oars. Using an opaque projector, copy a favorite character from Kenneth Grahame's classic about "messing about in boats," or from another good boating book, such as Maurice Sendak's *Where the Wild Things Are* (New York: Harper & Row Junior Books, 1984). Create from collage or draw on a single piece of paper. Put a fishing line in the character's hand or a flask of something good to drink and a hearty sandwich. And then have a cup of tea while book browsers devour your new display.

Fig. 60.

Fig. 61.

7

FOLKLORE AND STORYTELLING

To focus attention on folklore, mythology, or fairy tales, try building a display around a storyteller or an open book. In the design that follows, both are used, along with a few other characters which may or may not be included in the final product (figure 62).

The book becomes a three-dimensional object that stands out from the background through a very simple process of folding and pinning, while the characters achieve movement through cutouts and collage. You may choose to use only the book itself or the book and the storyteller. If there is space, however, include the child and at least one of the animals. Look through your growing file of veteran display characters to see if anything there will suit this display.

Begin, of course, by determining the space available, the larger the better. Think, too, in terms of vibrant color, especially earthy tones of green and brown, also sky blues and grays. Define your display space with the basic rectangle, using commercially prepared poster papers laid end-to-end or lengths of paper from a roll. Once this is done, you may choose to place a narrow border around it, using motifs from European or American folk art, such as stenciled patterns, stylized animal shapes, leaves, or Amish-style dolls.

Break the monotony of the rectangle by cutting out the "cloud-bubble" from one or more pieces of white paper. The rectangle still provides the basic structure of the display, but the cartoon bubble and the characters themselves will make slight incursions over the border to create a feeling of movement and freedom.

The open storybook is the centerpiece of this display; the other characters are placed around it. The symbolism here is obvious, since you are trying to promote the folklore collection; but, because the cartoon bubble provides the background for the book and shows that the storyteller is actually reading *from* the book, the serious bulletin board watcher may infer that he himself could enjoy a similar story by looking at the books on the shelf.

White or off-white paper is best for the pages of the book. It is essential that this paper be pliable, though the "binding" which shows on all sides could be of heavy poster paper. Cut off four equal lengths of paper from a roll, or use oaktag (figure 63). Fold these lengths in half so that when they are opened they look like the pages from a book. On the middle spread, write, in large letters with a felt-tip pen, the beginning of a tale, from either your own imagination or one of the books on the shelf.

Fig. 62.

From a piece of dark-colored paper slightly larger than the white pages, cut out the binding, and if you wish, texture it with dots and squiggles from a felt-tip pen to simulate leather. You may put the book together on a flat surface before attaching the entire thing to the wall, or you may wish to assemble the book bit by bit on the display itself. You may prefer to place the book precisely horizontal, parallel with the borders of the background rectangle, but observers probably will be more satisfied if the book is slightly askew, as shown in the illustration.

A ribbon-style bookmark will add to the effect of venerable age: if placed over the middle spread, it can dangle loosely, catching occasional breezes for additional movement, but it is also effective when tucked between the top page and those beneath it, so that it dangles from the bottom.

To build up the three-dimensional look, place the pages in the middle of the binding, stapling them together at least twice in the "gutter" or fold. Then move the outside edges of the pages slightly toward the center, creating the effect of a fat, open, and quite antique tome. Experiment with these pages before fixing them permanently. Staple the outside edges of the very bottom page in place at the corners, giving that page the shallowest billow. Each succeeding page should be stapled in the same way, but the outside edges must be moved slightly nearer the center each time and stapled, *not* to the

Making the Book

1. Make the pages from four equal lengths of paper. Fold them neatly in half.

2. Make the book cover from a slightly larger piece of colored paper, cutting it to resemble an old leather binding.

3. Make a ribbon bookmark to insert between the pages, or to place prominently over the center fold.

4. Attach the cover to the display. Then pin or staple the four pages to the cover, increasing the curve of each successive page to give the effect of a curling, open book.

Pin, staple or glue on the "x"

OPTIONAL: Write the opening lines of a local folk tale on the centerfold before mounting the book; or use the verse and chorus of a folksong; or write the details of a folk event or exhibition.

Side profile of mounted book.

Fig. 63.

binding, but only to the page immediately beneath it so that the book appears full, with more pages than are actually there.

If you wish to add further illusions of age to the book, fold some of the corners up, make tears, either real ones or in ink, and slightly crumple the edges of the pages.

Next, make the storyteller, since he is the most complicated of the characters (figure 64). Naturally, you may use any color scheme you choose: earthy, bold, bright, or calm. You may start with any of his various parts, but it is logical to begin with the torso since, as you cut the pieces out, it is helpful to place them on a flat surface in exactly the same positions which they will later enjoy on the display. Make the storyteller, the child, and the other characters with collage, much as American illustrator Ezra Jack Keats has used effectively in his *Snowy Day* (New York: Viking, 1962).

Having drawn the torso on your sheet(s) of paper, and cut it out, move on to the trousers, sleeves, and other garments. You may choose to make the storyteller an Indian, in which case a turban would be more appropriate than the floppy hat. Other hats can create other characters: cloth caps, American Indian feathers, African plumes and animal skins, Rastafarian hats—the choice is virtually limitless, and should be determined by your own situation.

The storyteller sits on a closed book. You may make a book which shows the bottom end, as in this illustration, but if you need space to hint at the location of the folklore books in your library, classroom, shop, or room, make the spine of the book face outward. Not only can you write a title thereon, but also a library or other classification number or other directional information.

The dog is the most complicated of the remaining figures, but by starting with the hind legs (figure 65), adding then the chest and forelegs, lower jaw and head, ears, eyes, and nose, and tail, in that order, he will fit together easily. Make sure, however, that the blacks of the dog's eyes look *up* to the storyteller's face. Vary certain details to turn the dog from a cocker spaniel into the breed appropriate to your display.

The child can be boy or girl or indeterminate with a simple change of hairstyle; it is yours to decide. Begin with the torso and leg, adding the arm and head, background leg, socks and shoes, in that order. Slight feminization or masculinization of the clothing will help determine sex. As with the cocker spaniel, make certain that the child's eyes look *up* at the storyteller's face, whether you draw in the features or cut them from paper.

From your growing stockpile of lettering, select a "folksy" style, nothing too serious or sophisticated, to emphasize the warmth of folk literature. Depending upon the ages you wish to reach with this display, you may choose another headline, perhaps from a book title. For young children, perhaps "A Story! A Story!" or "Once Upon a Time ...." For added movement and texture, select one of the more flamboyant means of letter display: shadow box, suspended, simple shadow box, or raised.

You may wish to put a few folklore books beneath or near the display, along with an old-fashioned rocking chair and floor cushions to accommodate the real storyteller and audience when the time comes to put the scene into action. Taped music might be appropriate from time to time, especially since so many folk music cassettes are available now that one may choose bluegrass, Celtic harp, dulcimer, vocal, and many other varieties to add audio color.

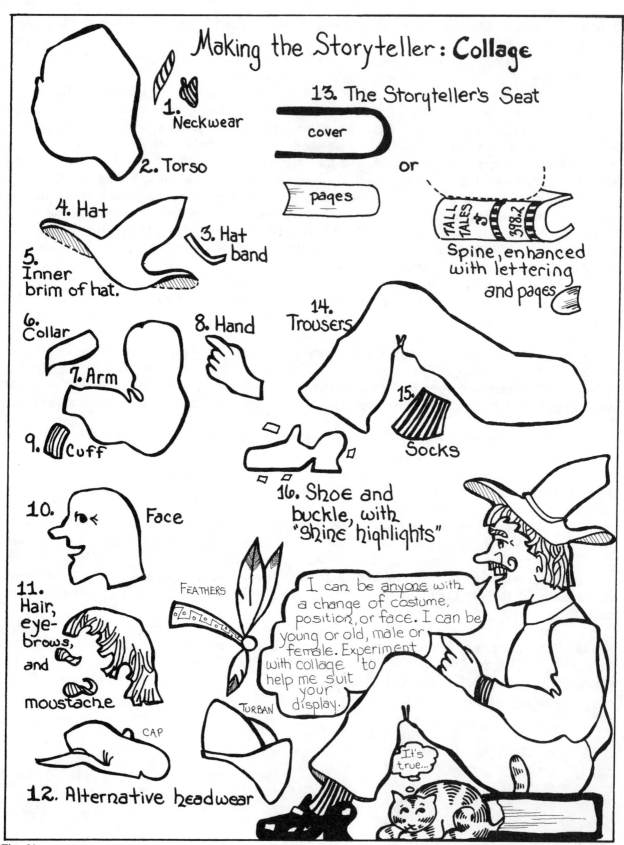

Fig. 64.

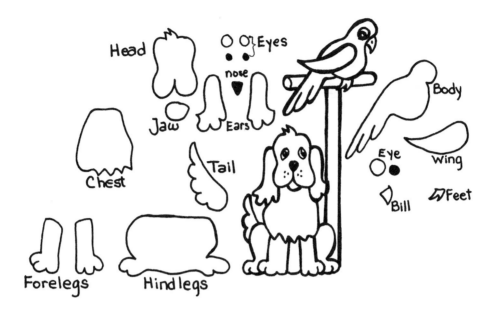

Fig. 65.

8

THE ENCHANTED FOREST

Contrary to the author's belief that displays must have headlines, a title actually does seem more appropriate for this silhouette of ancient trees and a rustic rail fence: *The Enchanted Forest* (figure 66). If you wish to include a title at all, you would do better to put it on a rusticated signpost apart from the actual display, as if the reader were about to walk down the leafy lane, looking-glass fashion, through the gate into the magic realm beyond.

To add interesting depth, create a theatrical flat of hanging branches to suspend from the ceiling in front of the main display itself (figures 67 and 68), in the style of shadow box or suspended lettering (page 12). Your title could be hung there among the branches, just as signposts guide walkers in the country.

This display also can be used to excellent effect on plate glass windows, so that the only cutting you have to do is the trees and fences themselves, as the glass provides the background. In fact, this rather magic effect can turn a library or classroom into an enchanted forest which you may never want to leave! The tranquility which this display imparts to any busy room is quite disarming. The first one the author made was intended to provide the setting for a middle school library class in the corner of a busy library. It stayed up for over two years when the original intention was to replace it after three months! After all, most displays lose their currency after a few weeks, and it is imperative that book promoters do their utmost to keep their stocks-in-trade moving with new and changing attractions. But this Enchanted Forest, when not in use as a reading area or classroom space for middle schoolers, was claimed by other library users, most notably seventeen- and eighteen-year-olds, as their own oasis. Talking was noticeably less here, too, since the enchanted silhouette created an ideal silent reading corner.

The woodland silhouette is perfect for promoting a collection of animal books, pioneer American fiction, or for advertising a summer reading program. Titles such as "Into the Wilderness," "Back to Nature," "Life of the Forest," or "Public Footpath—Enchanted Forest" blend easily into the fabric of this display.

Fig. 66.

If you plan to do storytelling, this display makes a nearly perfect setting, especially if you suspend some flats in front of the main panel, creating a snug forest clearing in which to nestle. Your own individuality can come to the fore, also, for if you plan to read *Bambi* by Felix Salten (New York: French & European Publications, 1981), it would be very appropriate to include a silhouette of a fawn beneath the trees. And if you include Robert Lawson's *Rabbit Hill* (New York: Viking, 1977), a group of silhouetted rabbits would be a natural addition. *Corvus the Crow* by Franklin Russell (Bristol, Fla.: Four Winds Press, 1972) demands one of his breed. Let your needs guide you to create your own fantasy woodland, with silhouettes of animals or plants or manmade objects that could be removed and replaced with others as needs dictate.

Suspend flats from the ceiling with pins or tape to give depth to the Enchanted Forest.

Support floor flats with cardboard braces disguised as shrubbery, or attach them to boxes full of good books.

Fig. 67.

The woodland will prove one of the most adaptable displays to make. If you do serialize *Rabbit Hill* over a period of readings beneath the curving arches of the Enchanted Forest, attach your warren of rabbits only when necessary. You may need the space at other times for the Bambi figure or for other creatures, ranging from gnomes to jack-o'-lanterns. By slightly gnarling the branches of your trees, you have a perfect Halloween glade, ripe for a witches' party. Instead of flying birds in the sky, make some bats or witches on broomsticks. Place a fierce black cat on the fence post. Call the place "Witchey Woods," if only for the season, after which it will magically revert to the enduring safety of the Enchanted Forest.

If your display area is plagued with a nasty central heating draft, capitalize on it with mobiles. Not only are they fun to watch, but children enjoy making their own. For the ghostly period of Halloween, make a *Bevy of Bats* (figure 69). Even if you don't have an overeager air circulation system, the paper figures will move whenever you walk beneath them. Hang with cotton thread from the ceiling at different heights, or refer to page 38 for more complex hanging methods. For other seasons, experiment with *Flights of Fowl*, such as a *Gaggle of Geese*.

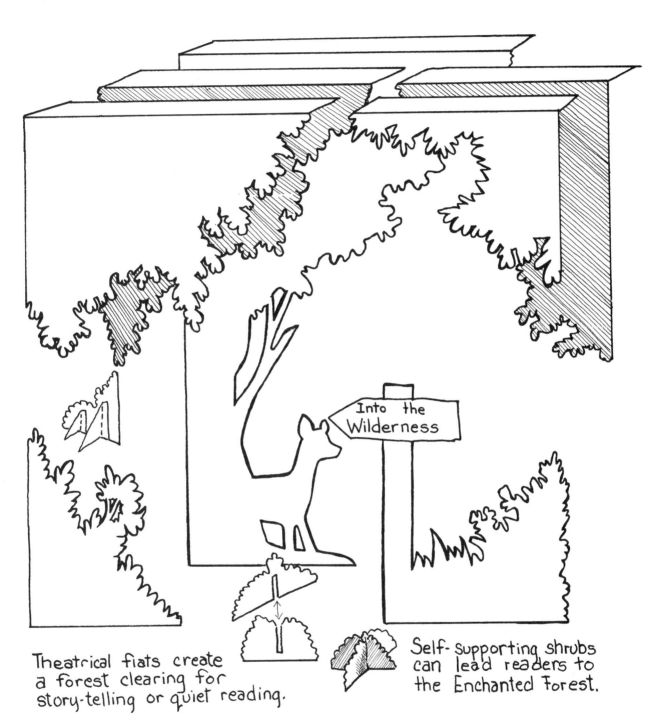

Theatrical fiats create a forest clearing for story-telling or quiet reading.

Self-supporting shrubs can lead readers to the Enchanted Forest.

Into the Wilderness

Fig. 68.

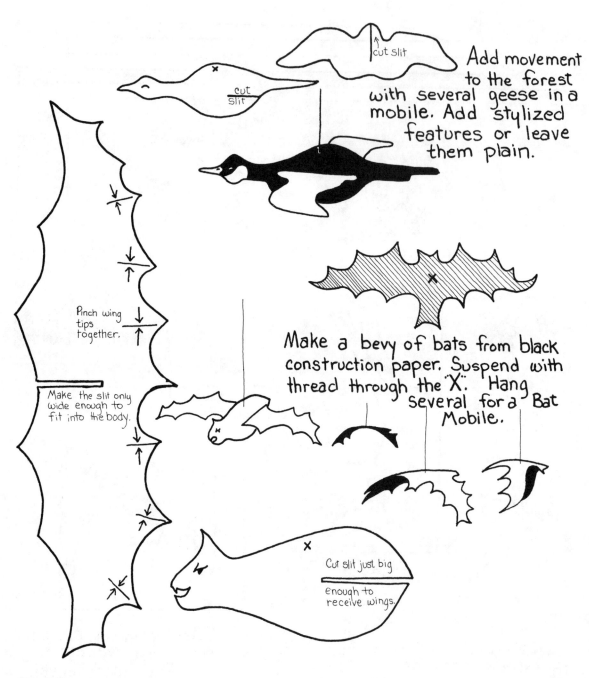

cut slit

cut slit

Add movement to the forest with several geese in a mobile. Add stylized features or leave them plain.

Make a bevy of bats from black construction paper. Suspend with thread through the "X". Hang several for a Bat Mobile.

Pinch wing tips together.

Make the slit only wide enough to fit into the body.

Cut slit just big enough to receive wings.

Fig. 69.

If you decide that a colorful display will better enhance your needs, plan a woodland like Enchanted Forest Number Two, which utilizes basic tones of brown, green, and blue, with some white cloud shapes and perhaps, a yellow flower or two. Some youngsters may more readily appreciate this type of woodland, but that conjecture is not borne out by experience. Everything is always subject to personal taste.

Flats must reflect the style of the background, of course, so create leafy patterns similar to those on the wall. You might even want to make as many as five or more layers of different sizes or fill your entire room with dangling boughs (figure 70).

Before selecting your color scheme, however, determine where you wish to erect the display. On a window? Use black paper, with no colors at all. Let the outside world provide that. On a wall? Again, black may be best, with a dark green background. Or make the silhouettes out of dark green paper

Fig. 70.

placed over a light green background. Keep the colors simple. Resist any temptation to color the display with realistic bark, grass, leaves, sky, and flowers, for this would not only be time-consuming, but would do much to destroy the tranquility and magic of the silhouette.

If you wish, the flats can contain birds and squirrels, in silhouette, holding placards with the titles of books, though this may tend toward fussiness and compete with the overall title. If there is floor space in front of the display, try placing freestanding silhouettes of shrubs and animals. These may be made of interlocking pieces of cardboard or supported by blocks of wood, flowerpots, or empty coffee cans, spray-painted black or matching the overall color of the display (figure 71). This will heighten the feeling that observers are walking into and beyond the enchanted woods.

Attach flats to old coffee cans, flower pots, stools or chairs to occupy floor space.

Fig. 71.

Very attractive freestanding animals can be made from cardboard or stiff construction paper. Again, interlocking pieces of card assure stability as well as adding dimension. Begin by drawing a frontal cartoon of the animal, omitting the forelegs (figure 72). In their place, draw two straight lines about one-third of the way up the figure. These will later be cut into slits to interlock with the individually cut legs. Draw the legs in proportion to the main figure, cut a slit in each one about halfway down from the top, and join the pieces together for a freestanding animal.

Since these animals may be viewed from all sides, they should be decorated front and back. In some cases, both sides may become the front by putting "paws" on what would otherwise be the back of the legs and by drawing on two faces, one on each side.

Animals may be made in other positions, too (figure 73). Avoid monotony by drawing some of the torsos in profile, adding four legs instead of two, unless, of course, they are sitting down, when only the forelegs are necessary. Sitting birds, despite their lack of visible legs, make ideal freestanding flats. Make wings to support the profile birds, folding them back into a V so that they closely hug the body, yet offer support. These animals and birds can also be made from plywood with a small electric jigsaw. Wooden specimens last much longer and take only a little more effort. Consult your local electrical tools supply shop or read the manufacturer's instructions on electric saw use, and experiment.

Fig. 72.

Make other animals from folded paper, with the torso and legs drawn in profile on one side (figure 74). Do not draw in a face or tail, since these will be added later. Fold the paper closely together, and cut out the animal's body and legs, which will be freestanding immediately. Then draw a face of the animal you have in mind, using some of the ideas in chapter 11. A curly tail is made from a narrowly cut, long, thin strip of lightweight paper. Run the blade of the scissors along it once rapidly to achieve a curl or twine the paper around a pencil, releasing it to achieve a similar effect.

Using the torso as a template, make several layers of wool or fur for the animal. Each layer should be large enough to cover the torso horizontally, but shorter than the layer immediately beneath it. Make them of different complementary colors for greater effect.

To ensure observer participation in this display, try this game: either on the hanging flats or on the freestanding silhouettes, create little animals with riddles or questions on their placards, based upon the books in which they appear. The floor flats are ideal for this activity, since you can put individual questions or riddles on strips of card and place them in the empty coffee cans (figure 75). In the can which supports a bunny silhouette, make several *Quip Strips* with riddles such as, "My name is Georgie! Who am I?" or "New folks a-coming! New folks a-coming! Why did I sing this song?" or "Mr. MacGregor chased me from his garden. Who am I?" There may not be enough room, however, to create silhouettes of all the animals or other characters in the books, so one figure can stand for several. Thus another Quip Strip can ask, "Who am I? I had to dress up as a washerwoman, although I am a gentleman!" or "My entire community had to flee the town dump to look for a new home. Who are we?" This can be done without representational characters offering a strong hint.

When a participant has answered a set number of Quip Strips correctly, writing his answers on his own permanent score sheet, he becomes eligible for a prize: a gold star beside his name on the class list on the wall, a badge, a certificate, extra credit in teacher's book, or some other treat at the end of the project.

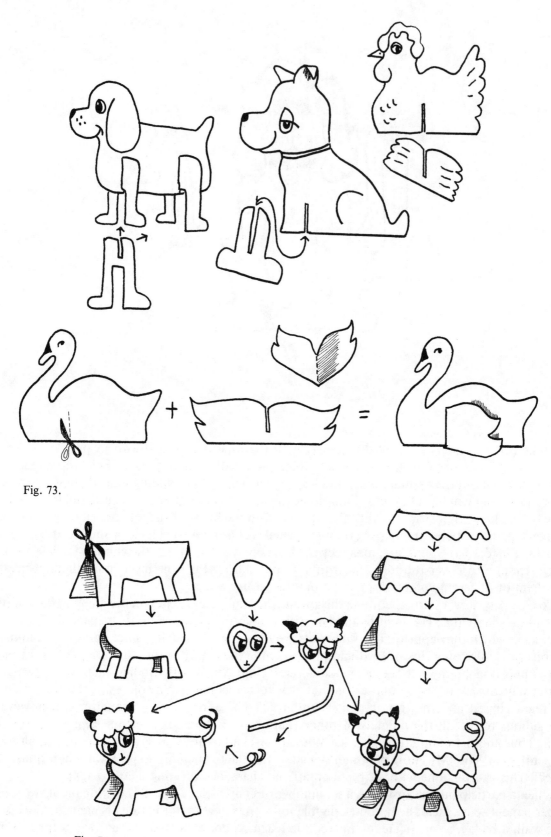

Fig. 73.

Fig. 74.

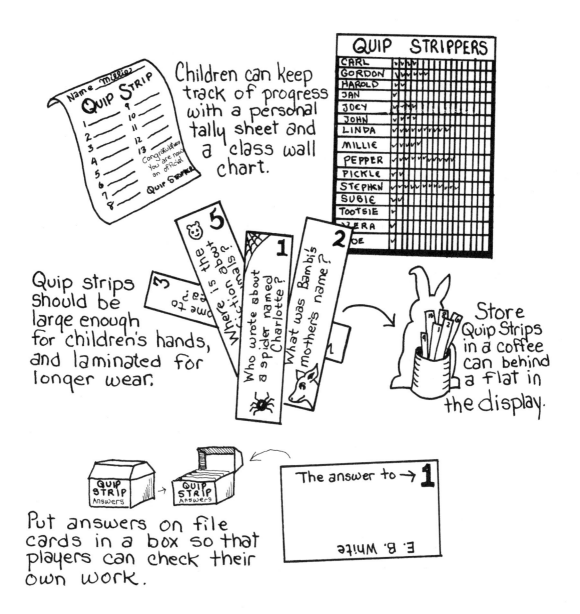

Fig. 75.

Variations on the game are innumerable. Some Quip Strips can ask a child to locate books in the library, giving their call number. Or they may ask the child to name the artist who drew the illustrations. Other questions could ask the child to do some research in biographical dictionaries to find out the author's or illustrator's birthday or to write a paragraph describing action in the story.

This display, when first used, covered an entire wall from ceiling to floor, a height of about eleven feet. To provide enough space around a chair for storytelling, the Enchanted Forest spread to a width of over ten feet. The only limitations which you will encounter are the amount of paper at your disposal and the availability of display space.

An equally enchanting forest can be made for Lilliputians on a tabletop, with everything much, much smaller. You can even put it all inside a corrugated box, much as you might make a model theater, a dollhouse, or a Fox Box (see page 32). Since many youngsters are already familiar with *dioramas* (shoebox scenes which illustrate a favorite passage from a story), they will want to help by making their favorite characters to go inside the miniature Enchanted Forest. If so, you may get a complete set of Uncle Remus, Snow White, or Rabbit Hill characters.

If storage presents a problem, it is better to build a folding diorama of stiff paper. This Enchanted Forest is magic not only because of its diminutive size, but also because of its structure: five or more scenery sheets, each resting inside accordion-pleated side panels, with successively smaller cutout holes toward the back. An added advantage is that, while only one frame is necessary, several settings can be developed on different themes or books and filed away when not in use.

Start with two side panels of stiff paper (figure 76). These could be anywhere from eight by ten to nine by twelve inches or larger. At intervals of one inch, draw a line from horizontal top to bottom. Fold along these lines to make accordion pleats.

Cut three more panels the same size as the side panels, but make these of corrugated cardboard. These will become the base, the back, and the proscenium arch. Beginning with the front, or proscenium, cut out an opening approximately one and a half inches from the top and sides, but going all the way to the bottom.

The proscenium can be decorated to look like a theater, covered with wallpaper, or painted a plain color, such as dark green or black. Dark or dull colors will not detract from the scenes inside.

With strong glue, join the side panels to the proscenium and to the back panel, which has not been cut into at all. Reinforce the bond with staples if necessary. Attach the base to the bottom of the back panel with cellophane tape, the heavier the quality, the better, since it will serve as a hinge when the theater is stored away. Similarly, a top panel or ceiling also could be attached, keeping out dust or inquisitive fingers, but reducing light. For special effects, the top panel could be made from colored acetate. Paint the floor green, dark brown, or neutral gray. Paint the back panel a neutral sky color or laminate with colored paper to reduce danger of warping.

When this framework is ready, the fun part begins. Decide on the theme: Enchanted Forest (which can be the backdrop for anything from "Bambi" to "Red Riding Hood" to Appalachian folk tales); City Sidewalk (for George Selden's *Cricket in Times Square* [New York: Dell, 1970] or E. L. Konigsburg's *From the Mixed-up Files of Mrs. Basil E. Frankweiler* [New York: Atheneum, 1967]); Farmyard (for E. B. White's *Charlotte's Web* [New York: Harper & Row Junior Books, 1952] or George Orwell's *Animal Farm* [New York: Harcourt Brace Jovanovich, 1954]); or anything else. Before actually drawing them on heavy card (or poster board), plan the scenery sheets, one at a time, on tracing paper, so that they can be placed one over the other, ensuring that each cutout gets smaller toward the backdrop. The scenery sheets must be the same size as the other panels so that they will nestle snugly into the accordion folds.

Other pieces may be added, such as (1) floor coverings: a path through the forest, a pavement, a sidewalk, a street, or a carpet, all made of paper and placed to fit inside the completed scenario; (2) upright properties: wheelbarrows, mangers, water barrels, mailboxes, or anything appropriate to the story or theme, made of folded paper or discarded household items such as cotton thread spools; and (3) characters from the books, cut from stiff paper and self-supporting with flaps or interlocking pieces.

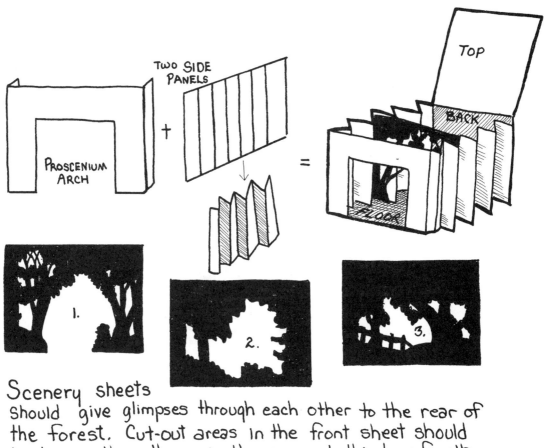

Scenery sheets
should give glimpses through each other to the rear of
the forest. Cut-out areas in the front sheet should
be larger than those in the second, third, or fourth.

Fig. 76.

Once the little theater, with its scenery flats and props and the books on display nearby, is completed, it will be time to make another, perhaps with the assistance of the art club, the children of a special class, or an interested colleague. When the display has temporarily lived its time, remove the scenery flats and paper properties, fold the base of the theater back-to-back against the back panel and push the accordion panels down. Can any other book display medium be stored away quite as easily?

Yes. There is one display which, if prizes were available for "Most Collapsible and Storable," would sweep the lot: the *Pop-up*. Not only is the Pop-up display three-dimensional, it also folds flat and has only one major drawback: it is hard to make. Elaborate construction and difficult maneuvering, however, are the lifeblood of true display-makers, whose patience and skill certainly will bear fruit here.

For a first attempt, select a simple design, with perhaps only one or two characters or pieces, each of which eventually will be attached to the cover sheet or to the unit immediately behind it. To illustrate very basic Pop-up procedure, make a little "cityscape" with simple geometric shapes, using scrap paper during practice attempts. Any paper will work, bar tissue or kitchen roll, so it is possible to achieve passable results with ordinary writing paper. Stiff construction paper or empty cereal cartons will give a stabler product.

To make the cityscape realistic from the start, try copying actual buildings from photographs or make a model drawing of a local school, library, or shop. If this seems premature, start with a cutout rectangle (figure 77), about four inches by two. Turn this into a building by drawing doors and windows in the right places, keeping in mind that for practice the best results will come from a tall, rather than a short, squat edifice. Reserve about one-quarter of an inch at the bottom for the flap which will later be glued to the cover sheet.

Fig. 77.

It will be necessary to put this building, along with its companions, into a folded piece of paper large enough to cover completely the finished scenario. Use a piece of paper, therefore, approximately ten by eight inches, folded exactly down the center until each side is five by eight. When making large Pop-ups for displays on walls and large tabletops, these cover sheets will be measured not in inches but in feet and the back of the fold may have to be scored first with an artist's knife.

In the cityscape, as in other Pop-up displays, the three-dimensional effect comes from the foreground leaping out from the background. Thus, part of the city must be drawn onto the inside back of the cover sheet (figure 78). Achieve this by drawing a simple broken line to give the impression of a city skyline. Add windows and doors, and perhaps shade in either the city or the sky to give the illusion of mass. It is important to do all the illustrations before assembling the Pop-up, because not only will it be difficult to do afterward, but any attempt to do so will destroy the carefully engineered construction. Do not use coloring materials that will repel glue; in fact, do not apply any color to the areas which will later support the braces and flaps.

Now that the background is completed, and the cutout building is ready, all that is left is the assembly. Place the cutout at an arbitrary distance from the centerfold. It may be helpful to draw a straight line parallel to and exactly one inch from the fold. Glue the flap precisely behind the line so that the cutout building is parallel to the fold. To ensure that the Pop-up will open to a perfect forty-five-degree angle, cut a piece of paper the same length as the distance between the model building and the centerfold, allowing for two small flaps at either end. Glue one of these flaps or tabs to the model building and the other to the back of the cover sheet, making certain that the cover sheet is open at a forty-five-degree angle. Now comes the crunch. Close the Pop-up very carefully and run a finger along the fold to make certain that it is closed as tightly as possible.

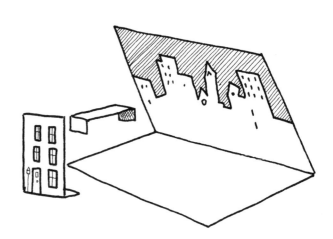

Fig. 78.

If everything has gone well, the Pop-up will open to reveal the beginnings of a three-dimensional city. Common mishaps are: (1) inaccurate placement of the foreground unit, which *must* be glued parallel to the centerfold; (2) overapplication of glue, which bubbles from beneath the flaps and sticks the entire construction to itself; and (3) inaccurate measurement of the bracing piece, either too long or too short, so that the foreground unit does not stand erect.

Complete the practice Pop-up by adding buildings or other units, such as trees, vehicles, or people, all applied in the same way. Remember to (1) keep taller units to the rear; (2) provide a bottom flap for each unit; and (3) make connecting or bracing pieces the same length as that between the unit and the piece to which it is to be fixed. Since the first building was tall, the second must be smaller if it is not to obliterate it. Make an individual dwelling house, about two inches high and one inch wide, adding a quarter of an inch at the bottom for the tab. Draw in details of the house and cut it out. Place it one-half inch in front of the original office building, making certain that it lies parallel to it. Glue the connecting bracer in place, close the cover sheet, and reopen. The three-dimensional city should be well on its way. To complete it, make additional units, placing smaller ones in front of the larger ones (figure 79).

Any display can be turned into a Pop-up. The only requisite is that the designer should draw the display in simple cartoon sketch first to see which items will be in the foreground and which can be drawn on the cover sheet. The ideas in figure 80 might motivate reading and an interest in books.

Fig. 79.

Fig. 80.

Don't be surprised when the youngsters start bringing in their own Pop-ups, Enchanted Forests, or miniature theaters, for once they have enjoyed yours, they may very well make their own. In fact, if you do make one of the tabletop versions, it could lead to the writing of scripts and the production of plays based on the books in the display; and you might even enjoy creative dramatics beneath the arches of the wall-size forest.

Apart from setting a tranquil stage for storytelling and daydreaming, the Pop-up is indeed a *working* display that may involve a few select members of a reading club, an entire class, or as many as you can provide books for. The display is adaptable for animal stories, wilderness and pioneer fiction, fantasy, and holiday reading programs, to name only a few.

RELATED IDEAS

Entice both children and adults into the Enchanted Forest and its books with *Amazing Crates*, proving that a rose by any other name might not smell so sweet. Use cardboard boxes, fruit crates, or bushel baskets, but call them *Amazing Crates*, paint them attractively, and fill them with *Crate Ideas* which can be anything from a new giveaway booklist, a plan for a model house (see page 121) or other craft, or leaflets for an upcoming puppet show or poetry reading—something connected to your book collection. Place the crates around the library or book space, at doors, in hallways, or at a reception desk. Label them and the handouts with the crate name: "Another *Crate* Idea from the high school library" or "*Crate* Gift Ideas for Christmas." Create other puns to give readers a laugh, and to make them look forward to coming into your book area. These crates are excellent year-round adjuncts to any book display, providing the means for uniform versatility that patrons will look forward to.

Turn the Enchanted Forest into *Stained Glass* by filling in open spaces with colored tissue craft paper. To simulate leaded windows, cut narrow strips of black oaktag into outlines for trees, wreaths, animals, or verbal messages. Use this method to catch light from outdoors, to cover ugly vistas, or to add a festive touch at Christmas, Easter, Chanukah, or Thanksgiving.

Sponsor an old-fashioned, country *Dinner-on-the-Grounds* inside or near the Enchanted Forest, based, of course, upon recipes found in your cookbook collection. Award prizes to the best chefs. Auction apple pies. Set a theme: picnics; portable high-energy food for backpackers; health foods; regional specialties—but insist that all recipes come from *your* cookery books. Have plenty of cleanup supplies handy, and lots of rubbish bins. *Everybody* loves food, so this idea will bring in the crowds.

Set up a small *Tent* in the Enchanted Forest as a haven for quiet reading. Add some cushions and a throw rug. Then establish rules for proper behavior so that young readers gain maximum benefit from this special indoor camping adventure.

9

PICTURE BOOKS
FOR ADULTS

An awareness of children's picture books as serious works of art for all ages is developing among some adults, so to speed the process, book people should plan specific displays toward a more universal appreciation of this form of literature and art. To read a good picture book is to reenter the innocence of childhood, to accept the impossible as matter-of-fact, and to enjoy some of the best artwork of the times.

Teachers and librarians, of all people, may be at fault for urging children to neglect picture books in favor of "meatier" stuff. In their haste to encourage the reading of written words, picture books are relegated to the nursery. They become lost to those who could develop an ever-deepening appreciation of their art and message.

Book displays are important tools for educating others about the many volumes currently in print. Thus, it is up to those who already know the great worth of picture books as works of literary and graphic art to teach others who may think of picture books as too elementary, if they think of them at all. Adults may quail at the idea of curling up with a "See Spot Run" thriller on the commuter train, as would any librarian or teacher. But unfortunately, many young adults and older people think all picture books are like the tedious readers they remember from their childhood. Happily, the truth is quite the opposite; the challenge lies in shattering long-held illusions about picture books so that adults will reopen themselves to them.

Extend the scope of the picture book by capitalizing upon the art of prominent illustrators. Adults and teenagers need to know that fifteen minutes with Maurice Sendak can be just as satisfying as half an hour engrossed in the latest bestseller. They need to see that a great picture book, like great poetry, leaves much unspoken and implies much more, very eloquently.

What kinds of displays will tell this story? Many avenues exist. Build a picture book "art gallery" to appeal to the lover of painting and drawing. Choose a theme, such as "Dogs," "Cats," "Pigs," or "Horses," and illustrate it with good picture books. Display the work of one artist, such as Maurice Sendak (whose dogs are famous); Charles Keeping (look at his many horses); Shirley Hughes or Graeme Oakley; and create a minibiographical showpiece.

Rather than outline several displays, it is necessary to look at only one in brief detail to get the general idea. Few authorities on the subject will dispute Maurice Sendak's position as reigning monarch of contemporary picture book art. Like Max in his *Where the Wild Things Are* (New York: Harper & Row Junior Books, 1984), Sendak is himself a king, not of the Wild Things, but certainly of the art of storytelling and drawing. His books are an ideal place to start in winning adult converts to the picture book as a legitimate artistic medium to be enjoyed and savored by everyone, regardless of age.

"Come to Where the Wild Things Are!" If this heading disturbs any innate grammatical harmonies, by all means change it, but it may work if Max is actually *saying* the heading in a cartoon bubble. By referring to the award-winning title in the heading, many adults may catch the allusion immediately, though if pressed to provide information about the artist and his work, they could not do so. The centerpiece of the display is, of course, Sendak's book, the now-classic American picture book in which young Max is sent to bed without any supper for being such a bundle of mischief.

Browsers among the Sendak books at the foot of the display may, indeed, come to where the Wild Things are simply by having been shown the way. Recent productions of the opera *L'amour des Tres Oranges* at Glyndebourne, England, with sets by Sendak, in addition to internationally broadcast operas based upon *Where the Wild Things Are* and *Higglety Pigglety Pop* (New York: Harper & Row Junior Books, 1967), may have paved the way for a display about the artist and his work. It may even be possible to include production notes, programs, photographs and drawings of the set and the production, thus pulling together his work aimed specifically at adult opera-goers and his writing for children. Clippings from the press or photocopies or microfiche reproductions of back issues will add immediacy and authority to such a display.

Relate children's books directly to adult activities throughout the year. During a major dog show, whether local or national, collect as many relevant picture books as possible, aiming them at a wide audience of children *and* adults. Use one of the artist's drawings of a dog as the basis of your own enlargement for this display. During the holiday season, when people's thoughts are naturally directed toward the decorative and artistic peculiarities of the period, display relevant picture books. Children's picture books can give adults a return ticket to Never-never land, an excursion to recapture lost innocence.

10

SCIENCE FICTION DISPLAYS

Time was when a sleek Flash Gordonian rocket conjured up the adventure and excitement of outer space and science fiction, but recent cinematic special effects have relegated that rather innocent mechanism to late-night television reruns. Today, travel into the universe is a bit more complicated. And little green men? A quaint idea destroyed forever when Tim Curry's sequined, cloaked, and fishnetted form first graced the stage of *The Rocky Horror Show*; an idea quickly buried as *Star Wars* and its sequels raged across the Silver Screen. How can a mere bulletin board compete with these exotic aural and visual presentations about alien life and science fiction? Fortunately, it doesn't have to. Science fiction is a readily moving commodity that doesn't have to rely on impetus from a librarian or a bookseller. It will prove interesting, nevertheless, to build some sci-fi displays, if only to show sci-fi addicts a few authors which they may have overlooked and to introduce novitiates to the fellowship.

When mounting a science fiction display, it is important to restrain the creative hand. It will certainly prove impossible to rival Hollywood, or even "Dr. Who," so this display must be dynamic in its form, color, headline, and overall simplicity; the books themselves must be the central attraction. A simple, catchy headline will appeal to avid readers as well as to newcomers to the genre. Go to the books for ideas. "Begin Your Space Odyssey Here" alludes to the complete title of *2001* (New York: New American Library, 1972), Arthur C. Clarke's now-classic favorite, and seems at once mysterious, alluring, and to the point. Let the black background (figure 81), represent the infinity of space, with a galaxy of white stars, planets, moons, and meteors, hinting at the infinity of imagination to be explored through the books.

By omitting any direct visual reference to spaceships, orbiting space stations, and alien beings, the display lets the reader form his own mental picture as he browses among the books, which will themselves abound with the creative endeavors of science fiction artists.

Some science fiction does not deal with human travel through space, but is set on terra firma. A clear sky at night on the display panel will not do justice to literature of this sort. You may want to represent a "Creature from the Black Lagoon," a Kraken, a Triffid, Dr. Who's faithful Tardis, or a futuristic city. But again, simplicity should override any attempt to reproduce cinematic monsters, or

Fig. 81.

the display may become funny rather than frightening. The vast store of film and book titles may provide headlines. "It Came from Outer Space" limits the scope of the display; "Step beyond Science" allows the observer to enter nearly any sort of science fiction book.

Closely linked to science fiction are horror and fantasy books. They all require readers to suspend, or perhaps to expand, their perceptions of the world around them, and to accept the supernatural or the humanly impossible as ordinary. To promote this type of fantasy, use one of the classic designs, such as the Clothesline (page 10) or the Sketch (page 12). Place a large white unicorn on a solid background. A very thick white border frames the unicorn, at the same time allowing it to escape or "bleed," as layout artists say. If drawing a unicorn is too difficult, trace a photograph of a horse (see page 4) and enlarge it by devising a grid or by using an opaque projector. The addition of a horn should pose no special problem. The unicorn display (figure 82) avoids representations of grotesque gnomes, dwarfs, and other humanoid creatures, yet evokes the core of what fantasy is all about. A headline might be, "Step through the Looking Glass." "Could It Really Happen?" asks the reader to provide his own answer.

For horror stories, provoke readers with the black cape of a vampire, from which leers the white face of Dracula himself, his white gloves beckoning. Tombstones at his feet could bear the title of the display: "Midnight Reading," "Spine Tinglers," or "Blood Chillers." To cap the effect, place the books in a long oblong box at the foot of the display, a candlestick at either end. A rubber bat from a novelty shop would add to the effect.

A larger heading, easier to read from a distance, could be placed above the vampire. "May I Tell Your Horror-scope?" he might ask. Or he could proclaim, "Welcome to My Terror-tory!" or "Bite into These Books!" To appeal to youngsters, who might not be ready for true works of horror, make the face of the Count a bit more lovable and change the heading to "I'm Bats about Books."

Suspend black yarn in front of the display to represent spider webs or use this simple and effective technique on its own (figure 83). Rather than knotting or tying cotton thread or yarn, take various lengths of black string and hang them in a straight line from the ceiling. The spider web effect is achieved by creating overlapping swags when the other end of the yarn is also fastened to the ceiling, either with tape or straight pins. Suspend a spider from a single piece of yarn, attached to the ceiling only.

Fig. 82.

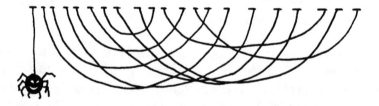

Fig. 83.

Make a three-dimensional spider from two pieces of heavy black card (or poster board). The body is roughly circular in shape, with a slit cut in halfway (figure 84). Draw a rectangle about as long as the body, with four long legs on each side. Cut a slit and add pincers and a mouth to make it fierce. Bend the legs at regular intervals to simulate jointed limbs, slip the two pieces together, and suspend by a thread or piece of yarn.

A perfectly acceptable flat spider can be made by adding legs to a circular or oval-shaped piece of paper. Draw on a face or cut out small pieces of colored paper to create a collage of eyes and mouth. The books themselves may rest safely beneath the web, either on a shelf or table or floor. But book jackets or drawings and cutouts of book shapes can be suspended from the ceiling, so that they appear to be caught in the web (figure 85). There are certain literary spiders known to dip into books and this display is just the place for that breed. Adapt the three-dimensional spider by making the pincers much

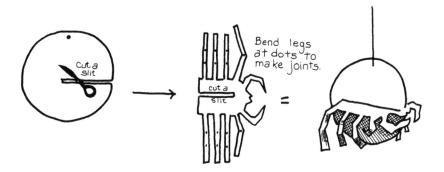

Fig. 84.

Fig. 85.

longer or at least long enough to hold a book, which can be glued to the pincers. Adapt a flat spider by extending the forelegs, including the book in the single piece of card from which the whole will be cut.

11

STOCK CHARACTERS

Surprisingly, the creation of good cartoon-type characters is so easy that even a first attempt will be good enough to put on display. Let any who doubt that complete a simple exercise: From a piece of any ordinary paper, cut out an oval (figure 86) large enough to represent a human head. To form the eyes, cut out two small circles from different colored paper, then two smaller circles of brightly colored paper to represent the irises. Finally, cut out two very small black circles. Place these three eye-pieces, one atop the other in ascending order, onto the face, which immediately begins to look full of life. Highlight the eyes with two tiny specks of white paper, placed off center on each iris.

To make hair, cut out a "mop" of any desirable color and place this on the top of the face. Eyebrows should be long "caterpillars," cut from the same paper as the hair.

With these pieces completed and assembled, you should have a cartoon face. Before gluing them down, however, try moving the eyebrows about at various angles to achieve different expressions. Also, move the mouth from side to side. Make the eyes look in different directions by moving the irises and pupils. Make astonished faces, happy faces, or frightened faces. Glue the features in place when you find the expression that suits your mood or display purpose.

This collage method can create any required expressions, from passivity to fierce anger by slight readjustment of shapes and position. Sleepiness or bored sophistication can be achieved by adding half-closed eyelids. A yawn, surprise, singing can be suggested by a long, oval-shaped mouth, positioned vertically. Anger results when the eyebrows are moved into a V close above the eyes. Try making the faces in figure 87. After cutting out various eyes, eyebrows, and mouths, mix them about to see how many expressions are possible.

To make other parts of the body, rely on the same basic shapes. A torso is really just a large rectangle, softened at the corners. Definition can be achieved by tapering or enlarging toward the waist. Arms are long sausages, to be made in one piece or two (figure 88). Hands present a special opportunity for creativity, for they can be represented as mitten shapes, without fingers, or with digits in place. Again, think of them as flexible sausages. Fingers can be made to grasp books or other objects, to point, or to make other gestures.

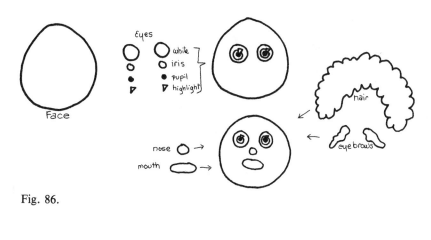

Fig. 86.

Fig. 87.

Legs are also large sausages in one or two sections. Ladies in long dresses or gentlemen in robes present no problems at all, as Kate Greenaway so well understood! Feet may be thought of as refined ovals, depending upon how the viewer is meant to see them. If seen from the front, feet are really the top halves of circles.

Animals, too, can be made from these stock shapes. The stock human face can become a bird (figure 89) with the addition of a bill and removal of the eyebrows. It can become a dog, bear, cat, or other mammal with the addition of appropriate muzzle and ears.

The only way to feel at ease as a display artist is to practice. The more oval faces one makes, the better one becomes. The more eyes, muzzles, noses, and other features one makes, the better the results. And since it is really so easy, with guaranteed success at the first attempt, perfection lies within the grasp of anyone who can wield scissors.

Amusing mobiles can be made from stock parts, as well (see figure 90). Refer to pages 38-46 for the basics in mobile construction and let your imagination lead the way. The difference in stock character

Fig. 88.

Bear   Cocker Spaniel   Cat   Rabbit   Bird

Fig. 89.

displays and stock character displays-as-mobiles is that the parts of the body are kept entirely separate in the mobiles so that they may swing freely. The facial oval, moreover, can be done away with entirely.

These faces and bodies may be hung separately or in units or they may be suspended from dowels or piano wire to make more sophisticated mobiles. In any case, each part must be made *in duplicate* so that identical doubles may be glued together over the suspending thread, eliminating the need to pierce holes in any of the paper. Book titles may be written on the books or use catchy phrases, such as "I'm Strung Out about Reading!" or "Pull Yourself Together with a Good Book," or something appropriate for the time and place.

Fig. 90.

Fairy tales lend themselves easily to stock character creations; they should not be neglected by book promoters who want displays that will attract not only children, but teenagers and adults, too (figure 91). Few sources are as rich in character stereotypes, magic objects, and genuine emotion as are these old stories. Walt Disney knew this when he stripped away all but the most basic cartoon outlines in his classic adaptations of *Snow White* and *Cinderella*, reducing much of the detail into instantly recognizable forms of good and evil. Formerly considered corruptive and inferior, but still loved by children, Disney's animated fairy tales are famous the world over for their simple, evocative portrayal of human drama. Display artists can use the old tales just as Disney and his successors have done, knowing that most passersby will pause to look at simple cartoon animals and won't be at all surprised to see those animals reading books.

Fig. 91.

Inspired by Disney's fairy godmothers, handsome princes, and winsome animals, the book promoter can assimilate these characters into displays, assured that nearly every observer will recognize them. While Disney characters may be more popular than any others, book promoters should feel free to adapt illustrations of other artists (obtain permission, if necessary) or to make their own originals from stock. Gradually, a file of book characters will enable the displayer to adapt what was originally an Uncle Remus Brer Fox into a Wicked Wolf or a rustic storyteller into a woodsman.

Many of the old tales rely upon formulas, which, if repeated often enough or in the right sequence, ensure apparitional appearances, magical occurrences, miraculous deliverances, or happiness everafter. Others are simply preludes of cinematic themes introducing characters or events: no one says "Fee Fie Fo Fum" except the Giant; no one can hear the music which introduces *Gone with the Wind* without thinking of Tara.

The repetitive phrases make excellent headlines for displays. Paraphrase the Giant's rhyme: "Fee Fie Fo Fum! I Read a Book about Paddington!" The display could feature the Giant engrossed in one of the Paddington Bear books, perhaps with Paddington and the Golden Goose sitting on his knee. And how about these:

The Three Bears

This bed is too soft
This bed is too hard
This bed is just right!

becomes

This book is too short (or easy)
This book is too long (or hard)
This book is just right!

Red Riding Hood

What big teeth you have!
The better to eat you with!

becomes

What big eyes you have!
The better to read these good books!

Three Little Pigs

I'll huff and I'll puff,
and I'll blow your house in!

Not by the hair on my
chinny-chin-chin!

becomes

I'll huff and I'll puff,
And I'll blow your house in!

Wait till I've
finished my book!

Snow White

Mirror, mirror on the wall,
Who is fairest of them all?

becomes

Mirror, mirror on the wall,
Which is the best book of them all?

Or

Hi-ho, hi-ho,
It's off to work we go!

becomes

Hi-ho, hi-ho,
A-reading we will go!

Fairy tales abound in magic words, superhuman osculations, and other literally fantastic paraphernalia too familiar to recount. These lend themselves to displays, if only for decoration. A genie emerging from his oil lamp might urge passersby to join his magic carpet express by reading one of his books. A comic display for teenagers or adults might feature the handsome prince giving the kiss of life to Snow White or Sleeping Beauty. The headline? "Bored? Give Yourself the Kiss of Life with One of These Great Books!" At Halloween a magic broomstick might whoosh readers to Bookland, where nobody is *ever* bored.

More recent tales incorporating features of the fairy stories also can inspire book displays. In Wonderland, Alice was offered magic drinks and met quite fantastic creatures (Lewis Carroll, *Alice in Wonderland* [Cutchoque, N.Y.: Buccaneer Books, 1981]). The White Rabbit might be late for an important date with a book. The Mad Hatter might offer readers a seat at his tea table, saying "Won't You Join Me in a Good Book?" A stream of small books pours from the tea pot instead of the expected beverage. When Dorothy journeyed so suddenly into Oz, she was given some magic slippers. They might inspire readers to embark on a journey down the yellow-brick road of good literature. When James stumbled upon his phenomenal peach seed, no end of trouble and delight ensued. Aunt Spiker might enjoin youngsters to enjoy a book with her.

Drawing the characters, if they are based upon those found in the books, can be simplified by using an opaque projector to enlarge the original illustrations. Thus, Alice can be the *real* Alice and Mickey Mouse can be the authentic one. Yet, stereotyped charming princes, wicked stepmothers, and blonde damsels abound; the skillful collage-maker will be able to reproduce them from items available in his burgeoning display file.

RELATED IDEAS

Organize a *Dress-up Day*. Award token prizes to everyone who appears as a character from a fairy tale. Enlarge the scope of the event by encouraging readers to dress up as a character from any book they have enjoyed.

During the parade of characters, participants can perform dramatic readings or improvisations from the books upon which they have based their costumes. Involve others in coaching young readers toward dramatic excellence so that the costume parade becomes a theater festival.

Invite a magician to perform during a *Fairy Tale Festival*, along with musicians, cartoon video shows, art contests, and tall tale telling. Play "Twenty Questions," either with costumed characters or with anyone who wants to be "it." One person assumes that he is a literary character, while the rest of the players try to identify him by asking questions which may be answered by yes or no. If the "character" answers yes, the player may have another question, but if the answer is no, the next player in turn may question the character. If after twenty questions, no one can guess the literary identity of "it," award a small prize to the character, and give someone else a turn.

12

ALL-SEASON DISPLAYS

If time does not permit a succession of varied displays, avoid the temptation to leave one exhibition on view too long. People just won't bother to look at it and the display will soon flag. The solution is to build a display for all seasons.

Careful planning before construction begins is very important, for this display may remain in position for up to a year or more, but with well-thought-out additions, deletions, and rearrangements during that time, it will convey messages, moods, seasons, and books. The display illustrating this is one which served as a Christmas book exhibition, a January ski holiday/winter sports exhibition, and a spring/Easter display, with minimal, but interesting, rearrangements.

The initial idea came from a splendid Arthur Rackham illustration in Clement C. Moore's *The Night Before Christmas* (Philadelphia: J. B. Lippincott, n.d.). The illustration depicted a snow-covered fir forest through which Father Christmas coursed on his reindeer-powered sled. The simplicity of the black-and-white illustration seemed perfect for a large wall space in a school library, in the middle of which was a pegboard about five by three feet wide. And perfect it proved, since the background was nothing more than successive strips of white butcher paper stapled to the wall until the entire area was covered. As in the Rackham engraving, this would serve as both sky and snow-covered ground.

Avoiding the traditional Christmas reds and greens, as did Rackham in this instance, the trees were made from black construction paper, enlarged freehand from the originals. (To use the grid method, trace over the originals onto thin paper. Make your own grid over it, then draw the final product onto an enlarged grid pattern.) Finally, the elfin figures of Santa and his team were made, also in black silhouette, with a cocker spaniel in hot pursuit added (figure 92). Rackham would have heartily approved.

Since white paper covered over the rather ugly outcropping of pegboard, it was possible to insert commercially manufactured metal book supports into the board by touch and feel, so that in the display, the recommended books seemed to land in the middle of the snow. When readers selected books from the display, others were put in their place. When the supply was nearly exhausted, the empty supports were removed.

113

Fig. 92.

This display had no heading or title. In the circumstances, a title would have been redundant, for the display was obviously about Christmas. The black-and-white spoke more eloquently than many brightly colored lights and tinseled trees. After Christmas, Saint Nicholas and the spaniel were removed from the display, as were the Christmas books. In place of the Saint, a large skier emerged (see page 5), sailing down the slope. He was dressed in colorful attire, so that he stood out brightly from the black silhouettes of the trees, emphasizing that the display had changed. Onto the pegboard were placed an assortment of books about winter sports, both fiction and nonfiction.

As the weather warmed and crocuses began to appear in the park, so too did early spring flowers start to sprout in the display, from which the skier had been removed. The flowers came slowly at first, but one day the students arrived to find a fir forest in the height of spring glory. Before that, the peculiarly American rodent, the Groundhog, had appeared in the snow on February 2 to see his shadow. Two weeks later, the display sported giant Valentine hearts in brilliant red, with a set of minimobiles (page 39) swinging in front. With the spring flowers came black silhouettes of deer, birds, and small woodland animals.

From time to time, various headings would appear. For the skier, a small heading proclaimed, "Get in Shape for the Slopes." Another possibility was "Après ski? Les livres!" The Groundhog Day heading asked, "Will He See His Shadow?" and the books related to American folklore.

For Valentine's Day, the heading was "Books to Win Your Heart," and the books included not only love stories, but also two volumes tracing the history of the season. A bibliography accompanied this display in the form of a Valentine bookmark.

Flowers began appearing soon after Valentine's Day, with the legend "Perfect Weather for Reading." This title lent itself to a display of all sorts of attractively jacketed books. As Easter approached, more flowers appeared, along with the animals, especially bunnies, colorful Easter eggs, and a selection of seasonal, craft, and animal books.

Through it all, the black fir trees remained, as fresh as when they began. The display lasted from the first of December to the end of April, and while its permutations may sound like hard work, be assured that much time and labor were saved.

Part III | Expanding the Book Display Concept

13

DISPLAYS TO MAKE
WITH CHILDREN

The displays presented so far were not really intended for construction "by committee," since it seems easier in the long run to design and execute them alone. It is appropriate to include children as helpers, however, when (1) they have chosen the books for the display; (2) their own artwork is available to be incorporated easily into the display; or (3) the adult has the time to instruct and guide them carefully in putting the unit together. Ordinarily, the adult will design the display, assigning various parts to an entire class or group, while seeing that the whole comes together satisfactorily.

THE READING TREE

The following display uses a simple template readily available for free. The resulting device can be adapted for numerous effects; in fact, the children will probably think of several not included here. This template is the human hand. The children will trace around it on colored paper, then cut out and assemble it many different ways: onto a framework of branches to make a *Reading Tree*, around a huge circle to make a Christmas wreath, onto the head of a deer to make antlers, or onto the back and sides of a fish to make fins. The idea easily adapts to sea serpent scales, flower petals, and many other things.

To make a *Reading Tree* (figure 93), provide the students with a basic tree trunk and branches. The height and width is up to you, governed by the space available. Put the trunk onto the display area, either on a solid color background or directly onto a plain wall. Several units of literary study can be worked into the theme, such as the children's favorite books, books with a strong character, books by authors from particular regions or countries, books about a particular geographical area, animal, or season, historical fiction set in a particular epoch, and so forth. The students make leaves representing titles they have read, to be added to the tree when they have completed a book. At your discretion, they may write their names, the title of the book, the author, and a comment about the book on the leaf before hanging it on the tree.

119

Fig. 93.

Beneath the tree, a rustic signpost could welcome onlookers to the Reading Tree. Have the children come up with puns: "We Couldn't *Leave* These Books Alone," "This *Trunk* is Full of Books," or "*Branch* Out and Read!" A drawing of a small animal or a student, from the stock character file, could sit beneath the tree or perch among the branches with a cartoon bubble holding the title.

Leaves traced around the hand make excellent Christmas trees, too, when done in shades of green. Again, individual boughs, as they now become, can hold titles of books, but to avoid fussiness and overcrowding, have some of the children add large circular "baubles" to the tree made of brightly colored paper. Titles can be written on the baubles and on the presents beneath the tree (figure 94).

The same idea works for a Christmas wreath, shaped around a large circle on the wall. Start the hands at the bottom of the wreath, leaving room to attach a red ribbon without covering any of the hands completely. The hands should point in the same direction, upward, as they move up the wreath, leading the eye to the pinnacle where they meet. The hands should overlap like roof tiles, with each tier fanning out slightly to give a full, bushy effect. Some may prefer to start at the pinnacle and work down, but the results will be the same. Insert a few baubles occasionally, on which are written the titles of good books to read. A headline may be written inside the wreath, over the top, or beneath it. Consider making a ribbon-scroll to carry a heading. These wreaths work well with the holly wreaths (page 58) and with the holly wreath mobiles (page 60). They can be made large enough to cover a two-story wall or small enough to fit on an average-sized door.

To make an evergreen tree, put up an outline of a simple Christmas tree, either in solid green paper or with string attached to drawing pins on the wall. Have the children fill it in with boughs. The hand-boughs should all point downward and overlap like roof tiles, so it may be preferable to start at

Fig. 94.

the bottom. Rather than point all the boughs straight down, allow them to fan from the center slightly. The very top of the tree should be shaped with green paper into a point, or have the children crown their achievement with a star, an angel, or a bauble.

BUILD A MODEL VILLAGE

Children from age seven and up can build model villages as a book-related activity and to invite others to sample their favorite books. To make *Bookville*, the teacher will have to provide copies of the buildings (figures 95-100). They may be traced and photocopied, produced on an offset press, or enlarged using the grid method, so that a larger (and sturdier) village can be built of heavy paper. With small boxes, it is also possible to use the Fox Box method (page 33). The teacher also will need to provide a layout for the buildings, using one large sheet of heavy paper, preferably green to simulate grass, and scraps of other colors to make rivers, lakes, streets, pavements, and fields (figure 101).

The miniature will appeal to nearly everyone who sees it, and it will be fun for youngsters to move the completed houses and other buildings about on the layout to create their own arrangements. The children who make the houses will not be the only ones to enjoy playing with the model town if it is put in a position available to passersby.

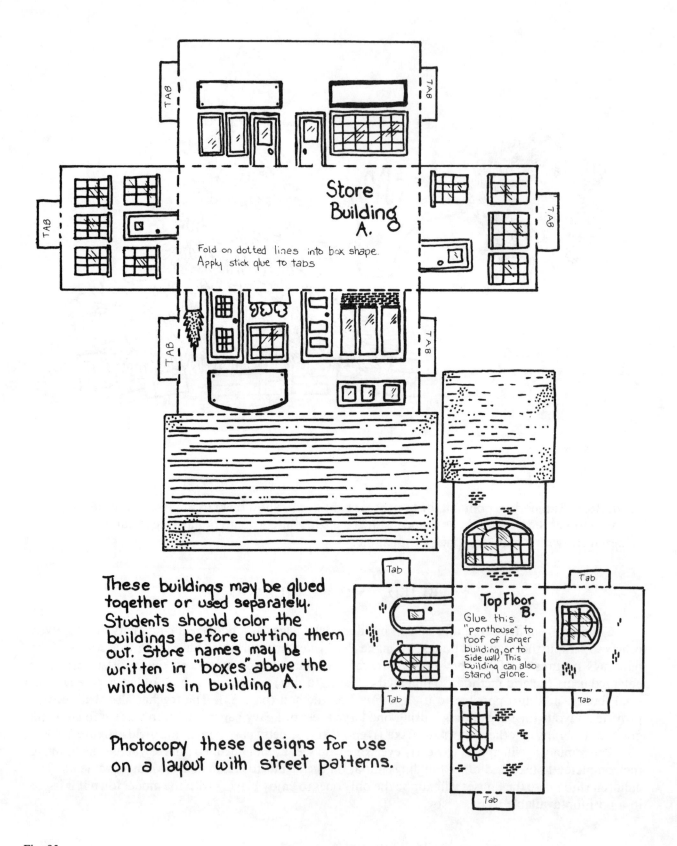

Store Building A.

Fold on dotted lines into box shape. Apply stick glue to tabs

These buildings may be glued together or used separately. Students should color the buildings before cutting them out. Store names may be written in "boxes" above the windows in building A.

Photocopy these designs for use on a layout with street patterns.

Top Floor B.

Glue this "penthouse" to roof of larger building, or to side wall. This building can also stand alone.

Fig. 95.

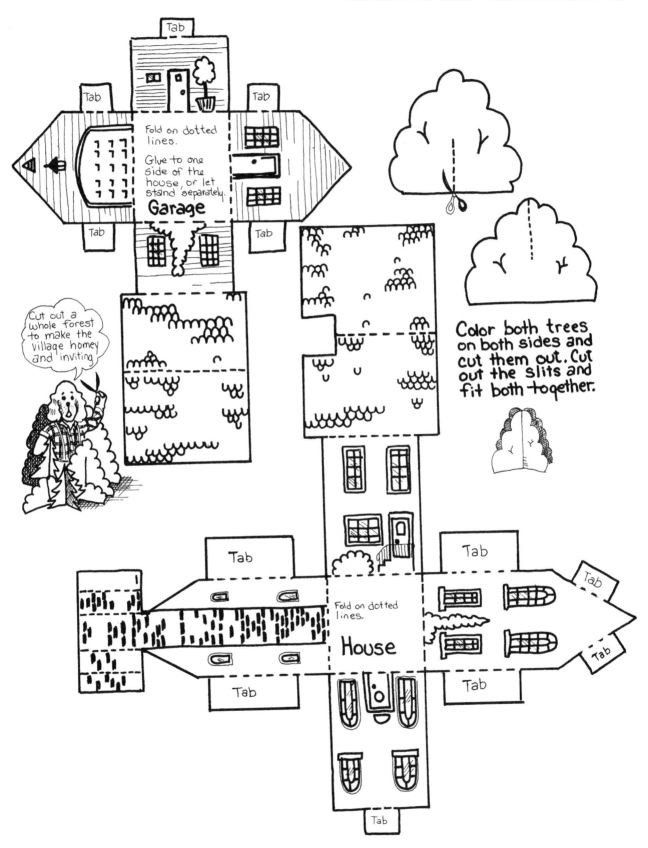

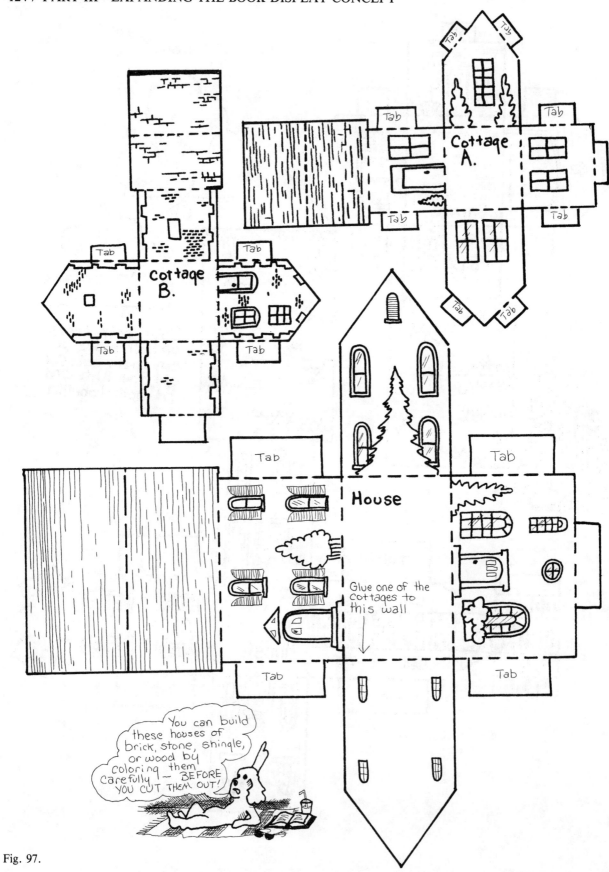

Fig. 97.

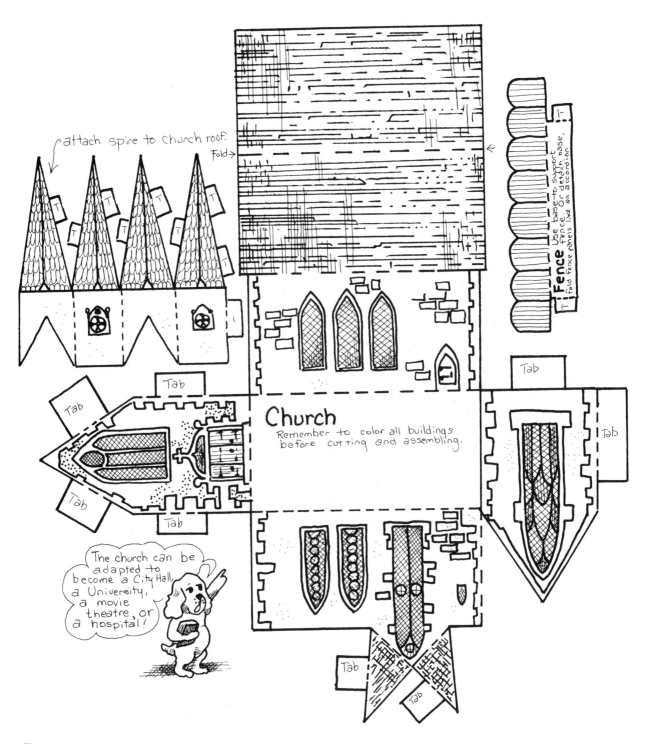

Fig. 98.

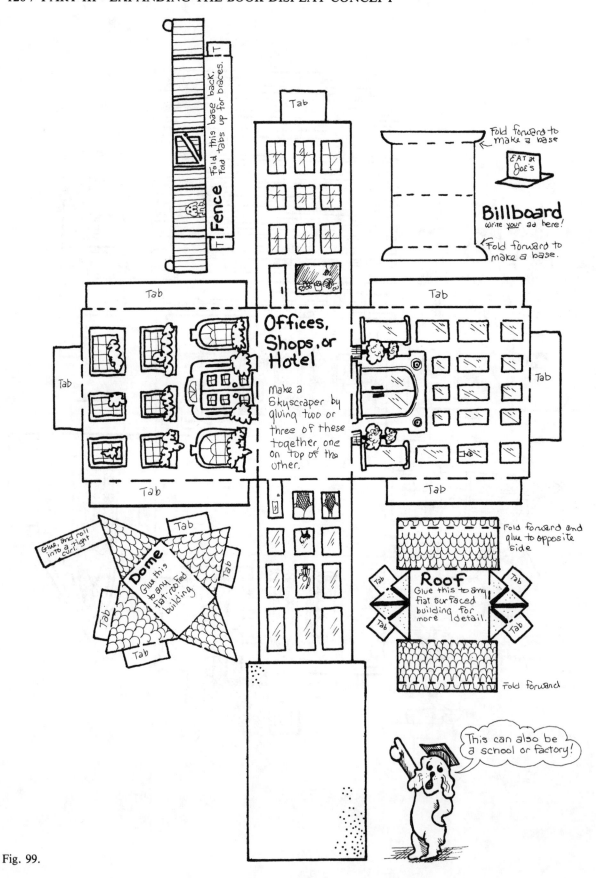

Fig. 99.

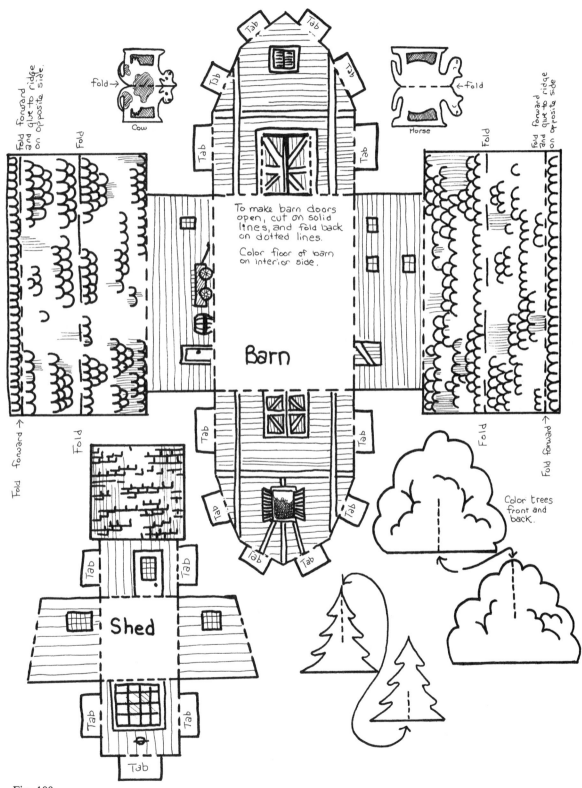

Fig. 100.

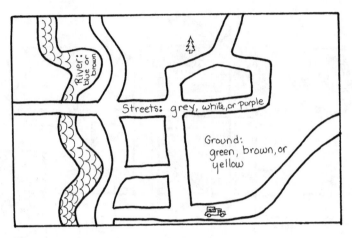

Fig. 101.

The village can become Bookville, Bookton, Bookingham, Reading Springs, or any other appropriate name. Various business establishments can take on the names of literary characters: who better to run the honey shop than Mr. Pooh? Mr. MacGregor's Garden Produce could be next door to W. Wonka's Chocolate Outlet Shop. Toad's Car Repair might be next to R. Cruso's Travel Agency. Join several houses together to make Bookingham Palace!

The children can choose the nature of their business and the names of the proprietors, provided they have a literary foundation. They will enjoy making private houses and other buildings to complete the village: the school, the church, the barn, the outbuildings, all of which can be named for structures in the books they read. Indeed, they may choose to build a village to represent one in their favorite book.

An activity to accompany the building of the village will aid others in discovering the literary allusions. With the help of the children constructing the town, make a "Visitor's Guide to Bookingham," in which questions (multiple choice, matching, or fill-in-the-blank) jog the memory to provide a pleasant literary excursion. The books used in the display should be available nearby, shelved or otherwise easily accessible.

To make other buildings of your own, plan from the ground up. Draw a parallelogram floor area, either square or rectangular, to the desired shape and size, and then make a cruciform, which, when cut and folded, will become the outside walls of the house (figure 102). To make the roof, extend one of the walls to just over twice the width of the floor. Remember to make tabs or flaps which later will be glued to the walls for stability.

After the children have made several of the models, which may be difficult for them without expert guidance, at least initially, they may feel confident enough to make one of their own design, based upon a local building or one in a book they are reading. Their efforts may not be especially neat, but they will enjoy the rather difficult exercise of planning and cutting.

While the cruciform floor plan centers around the floor, which is never seen in the display, a variation can omit the floor altogether, to have the building center around a side wall of the house (figure 103). Both methods produce the same results, but the inclusion of a floor does make the building more stable. It is easy to forget to draw in tabs or flaps, but they are essential for gluing the house together.

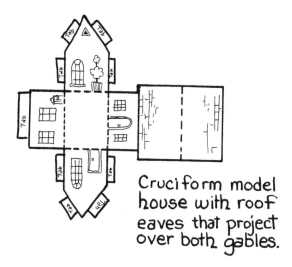

Cruciform model
house with roof
eaves that project
over both gables.

Fig. 102.

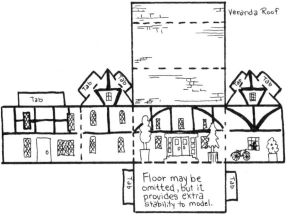

Veranda Roof

Floor may be omitted, but it provides extra stability to model.

Retain the floor for added strength in this model. Use toothpicks (cut to size) for porch posts to support veranda roof.

Fig. 103.

Build skyscrapers from flat-roofed buildings by stacking them one atop the other. A drop of glue will provide stability. Top them off with one of the house plans with a gabled roof.

For added interest in any of the buildings, cut out the door and window openings, using the method outlined for the Fox Box (page 34), and retaining the doors and shutters where appropriate. In the smaller model houses, this may prove too difficult, almost impossible for children's skills, yet the teacher may wish to add this extra touch.

To keep from peering into an empty paper house through the windows and doors, cut out a diorama for the interior. Cut out a piece of paper slightly wider than the wall behind which it will be placed. The extra width will provide a tab for folding and gluing at either end. Using the outside wall of the building as a template, lightly trace the door and window openings onto the second sheet (figure 104). Then sketch in curtains, plants, furniture, wallpaper, and other furnishings. Make the drawing

Cut door and window along
dotted lines so they will open.
Decorate inside of shutters
and door to match exterior.

These drawings show through
open door and window.

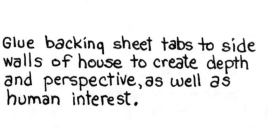

Glue backing sheet tabs to side
walls of house to create depth
and perspective, as well as
human interest.

Fig. 104.

larger than the actual door or window through which it will be viewed so that when it is seen diagonally, blank paper will not be visible. This technique, which gives depth to a building, works best with strong, stiff construction paper models and not with the small models shown here, unless great patience is involved.

BOOKWORM DISPLAY

Did someone say that bookworms are fusty bores? This one certainly isn't, and he gets longer everytime someone reads another book (figure 105)! The adult in charge should explain to the children that the bookworm can grow as large as wall or ceiling space allows. His body can loop back and forth to take advantage of every available foot. He can run across the top of bookshelves, across doors, even across tabletops and floors with light traffic. This bookworm does wonderful public relations for reading and books if he is allowed to sprawl down school corridors, in and out of classrooms, into the cafeteria, and even into the principal's office! He can grow for an entire school year or for a shorter period of time.

The adult provides a box of precut, brightly colored paper circles to be used by the children when they want to record a book they have read. The adult should begin the bookworm with a large head, cut from paper, and based upon the collage method (page 81). Add a book for the worm to read, too, either a dust jacket from a real book with some real gloves or mittens to hold it, an open book (page 80), or a one-dimensional drawing or collage.

Fig. 105.

This display not only attracts attention to itself, but also sparks interest in books as children see what their peers are reading. Usually, this sharing of literature leads to increased reading discoveries, for every segment of the bookworm is one reader's recommendation. Other themes may require something besides a bookworm. Anything that divides into segments will work just as well. A train could have a new car for every book read. A Thanksgiving turkey could grow an enormous tail with a new feather for every book. During March, celebrate the wind with a new kite in the sky for every new book read. Put a new animal in the jungle, a new tree in the forest, another brownie in the cookie jar, another star in the galaxy, or a new apple on the tree—one to mark each child's reading accomplishments.

FLY A FLAG TO BOOST A BOOK

Whether carried in a procession or flown from a mast, flags are emotional, symbolic, colorful, and beautiful. Flags are very ancient, used from earliest times to represent political, devotional, or collegiate affiliations. They can be used effectively to advertise books.

The smallest of the flags, the pennant, may be used individually or in ranks suspended from string to create a celebratory carnival of good reading. To make pennants, begin with a piece of paper about ten inches long and about eight inches wide, though these little flags may be made in any number of sizes and shapes (figure 106). Traditional pennants are triangular, though many variations exist. Some may end in inverted arrows, while others may look exactly like shields.

A single pennant may be put to good use on a crowded shelf, suspended from a dowel rod to attract attention to particular books or authors, one of whose names might appear on the flag. Tape the dowel into place and let the pennant do its work.

Whatever the shape of the paper pennant, it is necessary to have a flap or tab at the top in order to attach it to the dowel or to the string. Any paper will do, but beware of using felt-tip markers on lightweight, highly absorbent stock. The design will permeate the pennant, rendering the back unsightly. The problem may be overcome by gluing two pennants back-to-back, with a good design on both sides. If no words are used, the graphic design or logo may be traced on both sides of the paper, so that the pennant can be viewed from any angle.

Fig. 106.

Suspend yarn from a porous tile ceiling by wrapping the ends around two straight pins, which are then stuck at sharp angles into the tiles, far enough apart to give a soft curve. Since yarn stretches, plain twine or string may be preferable, if not as colorful. Attach as many pennants to the yarn as will fit. The pennants may be of varied colors or they can harmonize with a decorative or thematic plan, such as red-white-blues for historic fiction, red-green-whites for Christmas, and orange-blacks for Halloween. Some of the pennants could contain the titles of appropriate books, while others could bear a logo or motif, such as a holly leaf or evergreen tree, an open book, a witch or cat, or a circus clown (figure 107). This carnival of pennants is especially exciting for children to make as part of their reading program. To create a circus tent in a classroom or library, suspend several strands of string from as near the center of the room as possible, letting them fan out toward the walls in even lengths. The children may add a pennant for each book they read, writing their names and the name of the book and drawing an appropriate character. A wall display of circus clowns, acrobats, and animals taken from the stock characters (see page 106) would tie the "Carnival of Reading" together. When you take the display down, the children will have a collection of their artwork to take home to remind them of their reading.

Larger flags may be made of either paper or fabric, such as felt or burlap. These banners may be suspended from clothes hangers, dowels, or specially built rods. Paper banners are made in exactly the same way as pennants. To overcome any apprehension about their manufacture, think of them as portable bulletin boards which may be stored flat after use. Decorate these paper banners with cutout letters, stock characters, and drawings.

Felt banners look really magnificent, especially when the design has been highly simplified so that it may be enjoyed from a distance. Felt is preferable to burlap or other fabric because it does not need backing; it doesn't ravel; and it doesn't require hemming. Designs made from harmonizing colors of felt or other fabric may be glued to the banner, so no sewing is needed at all. Felt is also lightweight and may even be carried in a parade with no discomfort to the standard bearer.

Fig. 107.

Banners may be used on walls, as if they were traditional displays. They may be suspended from stairwells, ceilings, and window ledges. They may be borne in processions. To do any of these things, make a flap at the top, either gluing it safely together or stapling or sewing it closed like the hem of a curtain (figure 108).

To advertise books on crafts or rural folklife, children can make patchwork banners from the color photographs and advertisements in old magazines. Using commercially prepared plastic templates (usually the art department in an elementary school will have these or the mathematics teacher may use them to teach geometric shapes) or ones the display artist has made, the children can trace around them and cut out flowers, faces, fireworks, animals, or other items. Then, just as the artists of early America did, they can build a patchwork banner, except instead of sewing, they will use glue. Simple rectangles and squares will work well enough, or you may wish to experiment with more complex shapes, basing your designs on classic quilt patterns.

Fig. 108.

14

THE BOOK DISPLAY
AS LEARNING CENTER

Some people never will be persuaded that "learning centers" are one answer to today's educational needs, and it is not within the scope of this book to outline the fairly complicated methods of constructing them. Yet it is possible to build bulletin boards that do *more* than advertise books. It is not only possible, but imperative, under certain circumstances, to provide more than pretty decorations on the wall or floor space, for the book displayer will then offer educationally worthwhile learning activities.

ACTIVITY CENTER

The following idea, based upon greeting cards, can be adapted for any of several occasions: Christmas, Valentine's Day, Chanukah, Halloween, Easter, and even the long summer vacation. Each activity gives the participant an opportunity to learn more about books while making a gift for a friend; the overall display focuses on the books of the season. This sharing activity will work well for ages ten to thirteen or older, and can be modified to meet the needs and skills of younger ones.

In each instance, the display centers on a solid background, colored appropriately for the season. Christmas and Valentine's Day could be red; Halloween, orange and black; Easter, white or blue; summer vacation, any bright color. The headline could be the same for each: "Books to Read, A Project to Do," or "Read a Book, Share a Book."

The logo for the various seasons should be displayed prominently on the visual arena, whether it be a Christmas tree, a sheaf of corn, or a swimming pool, for the children may be able to copy or modify the design when they design their greeting card. Instructions may ask the students to come up with their own, different logo for the season, something unusual and original, or you may allow them to copy yours verbatim.

Given the name of a partner, either a fellow student in the same or a lower class, or a member of his or her family, the student will determine his or her partner's reading interests through observation. He or she will identify a subject that interests the partner, because "observation" can include interviews, questions, and "spying." The student can find books in the library, bookshop, or classroom, and finally present a list of those titles to the partner in a handmade greeting card. Depending upon the level of involvement, the student may even wish to buy a paperback copy of one of the books on the list and present it to the partner along with the card. This would be good public relations, if the student researched the interests of each member of his or her family and presented this special gift to them.

Besides the books, students will need access to colored paper, glue, scissors, watercolors or felt-tip pens, crayons, pencils, florists wire, and perhaps a template of the logo (figure 109). They will also need a working surface near the display and a place to store their work until it is completely finished.

This idea works very well when older students, for example teenagers, are paired with very young ones, such as eight- to ten-year-olds. Not only will the teenagers bring their considerable expertise to the project, but, moreover, they should enjoy the opportunity to act as Big Brother or Big Sister. School art departments may consider using this activity with their students, in cooperation with the school media center, giving academic credit as well as putting art to work.

This activity also works well when trying to teach certain aspects of library usage, such as location of materials. Using the greeting card they have been given, students on the receiving end may be required (or encouraged) to locate the specified books, either through the card catalog, verbal instruction, maps, or any combination of several techniques. In addition to finding their books, they will learn basic library layout (figure 110).

BUILD A READER'S FILE

This very small display can be used without any books nearby—on a tabletop, on a desk, or in a teacher's or librarian's office to which students have frequent access—or it can be put right in the middle of a library. The only requisites are a shoebox, some file cards, a small poster, and some ingenuity, followed by perseverance.

The *Reader's File* provides an excellent avenue for introducing youngsters to more and more books, but it also requires the devotion of the adult in charge. The idea is simple. From a lengthy questionnaire (see figure 111), given to participating students (an entire class, a club, or volunteers), the adult (teacher or librarian, or indeed, bookstore owner) learns what kinds of books appeal to each student. Based upon the student's responses in the set of questions, the adult locates books to recommend, a time-consuming process, but one which really works.

The questionnaire should be developed anew each time it is used, since local terminologies, slang, and interests may differ. The sample, however, provides a good basic format within which to work. The nonliterary questions are included for several reasons. First, a student may not state directly that he or she is interested in reading sports stories, yet may write that his or her favorite activity is soccer. It may be that he or she has yet to discover that there *are* good fiction books on his or her favorite sport and the librarian or teacher can show him or her new reading pleasures. The last question on the sample list isn't as preposterous as it may seem. Children who give very imaginative answers, answers which might even surprise the best fantasy writers, usually enjoy reading highly imaginative fiction—yet, they may not say that in so many words in answer to question 3 or 6.

The questionnaire is best filled out in a plenary session so that the adult can go over the questions orally, if needed, or answer questions of general interest. This normally takes half an hour.

Put instructions on the display board or on the table.
Have all work materials and art supplies at hand.
Samples of completed cards will fire imaginations!

Fig. 109.

The adult responds to the student on a three-by-five-inch card, which should be run through a printing press to avoid writing the basic instructions over and over again. If this is impossible, use a ditto stencil on plain paper, cut into three-by-five- or five-by-seven-inch sheets. When the student has filled up one card, staple another to it, so that at the end of a term or season, he or she will have an accurate record of his or her reading to take home.

On the back of this "Reader's Card" (see figure 111), the adult should keep at least two new titles all the time, so that whenever the student wishes to consult the card, there will be a recommendation on it. The adult may state that he or she will add a new title or two once a week, once a fortnight, or at other regular intervals. The cards are stored in the shoebox file, alphabetically or by group.

When the student consults the card, he or she should put a check by each title when he or she looks for it, just to let the adult know that he or she has tried it out. *Yet, the student should not be required to take every book written down by the adult; he or she should still be allowed to refuse any suggestion,* however disheartening this may prove to the adult. If the student refuses *every* book suggestion, then a conference should be called to iron out the problem, but the system works best when both parties are team-mates, not master and slave.

The finished card may be as
simple or as elaborate as the student
wishes, with cut-outs, collage, crayon
and pen drawings, a doggerel verse, and a book-list.

Fig. 110.

On the front of the Reader's Card, the student keeps a short record of the books he or she reads, whether or not they were recommended by the adult. A small space is available for comments, which usually turn out to be epithetic: "Yuck!" "Wow," "Great," or "Couldn't put it down." Eloquence is not required, yet this small space for written response can give clues to the child's progress.

If books in your collection are arranged in some particular order, such as alphabetically by author or title, by theme, by Dewey Decimal or other library classification system, or by publisher, then this information should be given in code beside the title on the back of the card. This will speed the independence of the library user and free the adult from having to find the book for the child.

Two shoeboxes will, in fact, be necessary for this project. One to store the questionnaires for easy reference and the other to store the Reader's Cards. The Reader's File should be attractively decorated so that it is easily recognizable. Perhaps a student or a group of students would like to cut pictures from a magazine to form a collage all around the box, preferably with a literary theme. If you prefer, cover it in plain colored paper. But be certain to give it a prominent title, perhaps jutting up from the rear wall of the box on sturdy card or poster board (figure 112).

File the cards by class, age, or by other organizational structure. If the group is small, there may be no need to arrange them at all. It is usually pointless to keep them alphabetically correct, unless the group itself is very small and *very* well disciplined for that chore. The adult will find that keeping the Reader's Cards in ABC order is an exercise in futility best given up, for the readers themselves will always be able to shuffle through them to find their own.

Reader's Questionnaire

Name _____ Age _____ Grade _____

Homeroom Teacher _____ Library Teacher _____

1. Give the titles of three books which you have enjoyed anytime during the past year. _____

_____

2. Are you reading a book now? _____ If so, what is it?_____

_____

3. Circle the four (or more!) kinds of stories you like best and put a star beside your very favorite:

Adventure	Animals	Books like Judy Blume's
Sports	Riddles	Puzzles
Love Stories	Biography	Stories about people who
School life	Fantasy	overcome handicaps
Fairy tales	Mystery	Teenage stories
Home, family	War	Ghosts, witches, supernatural
Science fiction	Magic	Stories set in times past
Spies, detectives	UFOs	
Crafts and models	Mechanical things, like	
Stories from foreign lands	trains, cars, airplanes	

4. Circle the type of book you prefer to read:

   Hardback   Paperback   No preference

5. Would you rather read a book that is:

   _____ one long story.   _____ a collection of separate, short stories.

6. Which do you prefer:

   _____ fiction   _____ nonfiction (what types?) _____

7. What is your favorite hobby? _____

8. What are your favorite games or sports? _____

_____

9. What kinds of work do you want to do when you grow up? _____

_____

10. Whose recommendations do you follow when selecting a book? _____

_____

11. Approximately how long do you spend reading each day? _____

_____

12. If you could have *one* pet, what would you choose? _____

13. What school subject do you like most? _____

      Least? _____

14. Out of all the places you have traveled, what did you like best? _____

_____

15. Of what have you ever made a collection? _____

16. How would you spend next Saturday if you could do exactly as you wished? _____

_____

Reader's Card

Name _____ Grade _____ Homeroom _____

      BOOKS I HAVE READ | COMMENTS

Fig. 111.

Fig. 112.

A small bulletin board, poster, or sandwich board may accompany this display, asking "Have You Checked Your Reader's Card Lately?" (figure 113). The display could take the form of the open book (page 80) or of any other forms of eye-catching artwork, such as the Pop-up (page 95) or the mobile (page 38).

Using one or several of the
display ideas in preceding chapters,
attract attention to the readers' file with
mobiles, pop-ups, or stationary signs made from poster-board.

Fig. 113.

POSTERS FOR PROMOTION

Finally, there is one last project which the adult may do alone or with a group of children: posters, an excellent advertising medium to tell people about books. Organize the kids into advertising teams, or sponsor a contest, with book tokens as prizes for the designers of the best posters. The posters could be displayed at strategic points in the school or elsewhere in the community, such as the public library, a church hall, a store window, or the doctor's office.

Basic rules apply to the making of good posters, without hampering at all the creativity of the artist. In fact, the rules provide a framework within which to make a readable, attractive work of art:

1. Single out one major point about the book, author, artist, or group of books you wish to advertise, such as "Alabama Writers—In Stock Now," or "Songbirds of Tennessee—Check These Great Books." Avoid including too much, for the casual reader can't take it all in and will miss the point entirely.

2. Keep the artwork simple and limit the use of colors. Choose a motif from the book or books you are advertising; for instance, for a promotion of local folk heritage books, put a small patchwork motif around the border of the poster; for a promotion of Michael Moorcock's science fiction, one comet or meteor streaking across the center of the poster would be eye-catching and complete. If students can use linoleum blocks to make their posters, so much the better, for in this medium, simplicity is everything.

3. Mention all vital details, which will vary according to the subject matter. Is one author's entire work being promoted? Then feature his name, of course, the titles of his books, a graphic motif, and location of the books. Is only one book being promoted? Feature the title, the author, the publisher, and where relevant, the price, library location, or a quote from a review (which often may be found on the book jacket). But don't say too much. A good poster will whet the appetite, not drown it with a glut of information, however good.

These three rules will help young artists focus their thoughts onto the essentials, and may save you a good deal of time later on.

The adult will need to provide the necessary supplies, such as paper, paste, and coloring materials, along with a few examples of professional advertisers' work. Left to their own invention, the students will make colorful, catchy posters about their favorite books or authors or about any other given literary theme.

For added incentive, ask a sponsoring organization, such as the PTA or a business firm, to undertake the publishing costs of the winning poster so that the designer can have the satisfaction of seeing his or her work displayed all over the community, maybe even in the newspaper. Turn the poster-making project into a public relations exercise by involving outside parties, many of whom will enjoy the opportunity to offer financial support for their *own* public relations.

If you do plan to make printed copies of the winning poster, then all entries should be done in black-and-white to keep costs down and to make it easy for the printer. If the poster-makers work in linocut or silk screening, instead of pen-and-ink or collage, the problem of reproduction is solved in your own art room.

AFTERWORD

Having come to the end, we are really only at the beginning, for as long as we believe in the power of books to improve the human condition, it is our challenge to induce people to read. As book promoters, we wear many hats: those of public relations experts, advertising agents, graphic artists, actors and actresses, musicians, storytellers, and counselors. Ours is truly a Joseph's coat of many colors, a mix-and-match outfit in which we must feel comfortable at all times to promote our product.

My wish is that the ideas in this book will be *your* springboard, *your* impetus; that your own projects in promoting books will far surpass the ones presented here; and that you will have as much fun promoting the love of good books as I have had.

BIBLIOGRAPHY

FURTHER READING

Displays and Bulletin Boards

Baeckler, V., and L. Larson. *Go, Pep, and Pop: Two Hundred and Fifty Tested Ideas for Lively Libraries.* New York: Unabashed Librarian, 1976.

Bowers, M. K. *Easy Bulletin Boards.* Metuchen, N.J.: Scarecrow Press, 1974.

Brown, J. C. *Cartoon Bulletin Boards.* Belmont, Calif.: Pitman Learning, 1971.

Coplan, K. *Effective Library Exhibitions.* 2d ed. Dobbs Ferry, N.Y.: Oceana, 1974.

Fuda, G. E., and E. L. Nelson. *The Display Specialist.* New York: McGraw-Hill, 1976.

Garvey, Mona. *Teaching Displays: Their Purpose, Construction, and Use.* Hamden, Conn.: Shoe String Press, 1972.

Hall, S., and B. Keith. *Three-D Bulletin Boards: Any Teacher Can.* New York: DOK Publications, 1974.

Jay, M. E. *Involvement Bulletin Boards and Other Motivational Reading Activities.* Hamden, Conn.: Shoe String Press, 1976.

Langholtz, E., and D. Ubinas. *Pickup Book of Cartoonstyle Illustrations.* New York: Arco Publishing, 1978.

Ruby, D. *Four-D Bulletin Boards That Teach.* Belmont, Calif.: Pitman Learning, 1960.

Salkin, J., and L. Gordon. *Orange Crate Art.* New York: Warner, 1976.

Learning Centers and Self-Motivated Educational Projects

Taylor, P. *The Kids' Whole Future Catalog.* New York: Random House, 1982.

Treasure Chest for Teachers: Services Available to Teachers and Schools. London: Schoolmaster Publishing Company, 1971.

Voight, R. C. *Invitation to Learning: The Learning Center Handbook.* Washington, D.C.: Acropolis Books, 1971.

Waters, D. *A Book of Projects.* London: Mills and Boon, 1972.

Wilkinson, C. E. *Educational Media and You.* Toronto: Educational Materials and Services, 1971.

Publicity and Public Relations

Dudley, J. *Promoting the Organization: A Guide to Low Budget Publicity.* New York: International Ideas, 1975.

Farlow, H. *Publicizing and Promoting Programs.* New York: McGraw-Hill, 1979.

Waters, K. *Publicize It with Pictures!* Hollywood, Calif.: Creative Book Company, 1979.

Watkins, J. C. *The One Hundred Greatest Advertisements, Who Wrote Them, and What They Did.* 2d ed. New York: Dover Press, 1959.

Readers and Books

Bamberger, R. *Promoting the Reading Habit.* New York: Unipub, 1975.

Cleary, F. D. *Discovering Books and Libraries.* 2d ed. New York: H. W. Wilson, 1977.

Hearne, B. *Choosing Books for Children: A Commonsense Guide.* New York: Delacorte, 1980.

Lindskoog, J., and Lindskoog, Kathryn. *How to Grow a Young Reader: A Parents' Guide to Children and Books.* Elgin, Ill.: David C. Cook, 1978.

Reasoner, C. F. *Releasing Children to Literature.* New York: Dell, 1976.

ANNOTATED LIST OF PERIODICALS WITH CREATIVE LAYOUTS

A cursory look through a comprehensive public library, bookstore, or supermarket will reveal a layout of colorful, interesting magazines. A reference book such as Ulrich's *International Periodicals Directory* (New York: R. R. Bowker) will mention so many magazines and periodicals that even the most dedicated reader may express amazement at the sheer number of weekly, monthly, and other periodical publications available throughout the world today. The following list, therefore, of twenty good, readable, watchable magazines, mostly from the United States and Great Britain, represents only a few which (1) are readily available, either by subscription, library, or news agent; (2) are interestingly and graphically arranged; (3) are good places to gain ideas for displays; and (4) represent the author's peculiar preferences. You will, no doubt, be able to mention a score of others which have been omitted here.

ARTnews. 122 E. 42 St, New York 10017.

Classy, smart, chic, with clean layout, it uses many of the standard forms, such as the Townscape and the Mosaic. Advertisements are also very uncluttered and inspirational.

British Heritage. Historical Times, Inc., 2245 Kohn Road, Harrisburg, Pennsylvania 17105.

This magazine has big, attractive layouts, using large photos with overlaid text. It has good drawings and interesting juxtaposition of text with illustrations.

Cotswold Life. English Country Magazines, Alma House, Rodney Road, Cheltenham, Gloucestershire, England.

Conservative, picture-postcard magazine, it has ideas for homey, country displays. Lovely photos of the best of English villages, thatched houses, age-old pubs, and rural life fill each issue.

Country Life. PIC Magazines, Ltd., Tower House, Southampton Street, London WC2E 9QX, England.

With luxurious color photos and dignified use of space and text, this magazine glorifies the British country house. The well-illustrated ads could blossom into wall-sized display ideas.

Creative Ideas for Living. 500 Office Park Drive, Birmingham, Alabama 35223.

This periodical boasts lively articles with well-placed illustrations. Although designed for the do-it-yourself enthusiast or amateur artist, this magazine offers many display ideas through its how-to articles, ads for craft supplies, and superb and attractive layout.

Early American Life. Historical Times, Inc., 2245 Kohn Road, Harrisburg, Pennsylvania 17105.

Graphics by draftsmen and layout by professional experts ensure that this colorful magazine is classically pleasing to its devoted readership. The layout is conservative and uncluttered. In addition, there are lots of well-designed small ads to study.

Ebony. Johnson Publishing, 820 S. Michigan Ave, Chicago, Illinois 60605.

A perennial classic, this magazine uses a tasteful, conservative layout, good photography, and excellent counterplay of illustration and text about black Americans.

Horizon. Boone, Inc., Drawer 2, Tuscaloosa, Alabama 35402.

An arts magazine with a good mix of conservative and exploratory layout, photography, and advertisements, it also provides inspirations for sports, dance, and other activity displays.

House and Garden. (Incorporating *Wine and Food Magazine*). Vogue House, Hanover Square, London WIR OAD, England; or 350 Madison Avenue, New York 10017.

A favorite of many designers and home decorators, this magazine combines glamor with easily enjoyed layout. It is perfect for the amateur layout designer to contemplate for inspirational ideas.

In Britain. British Tourist Authority, Head Office, 64 St. James Street, London SW1; or British Tourist Authority, 680 5th Avenue, New York 10019.

Perhaps the most famous and inviting of the British travel glossies, it features innovative layout, with lots of appealing photos. It is useful for gleaning ideas not only for historical displays, but also for architecture, literature, horticulture, food, travel, religion, and geography.

Norfolk Fair. R. F. Eastern, Ltd., 5 Grey Friars Road, Norwich NR1 1PR, Norfolk, England.

A small, but lovingly illustrated magazine devoted to this part of East Anglia, it has many good, colorful photos, well-arranged around the text. Folk life, crafts, cathedrals, castles, North Sea wildlife, and windmills are featured topics.

Popular Photography. Davis Publishing Company, 1 Park Avenue, New York 10016.

The title alone leads the display artist to expect clever layout and good photography, but the ads are also worth noticing for graphic ideas and layout suggestions.

Rolling Stone. 745 Fifth Avenue, New York 10022.

Is it a tabloid, or is it a magazine? Whatever, *Rolling Stone* is courageous in design, with enough ideas in one huge issue to keep the book promoter busy with his notebook for hours. It provides excellent coverage of the trendy world of pop culture, with good ads.

Seventeen. Triangle Communications, 850 3rd Avenue, New York 10022.

The lady among teenage girls' periodicals, it distinguishes itself with classy ads, chic photography and layout, and innovative graphics.

Southern Living. P.O. Box 2851, Birmingham, Alabama 35223.

This periodical prefers a conservative, no-nonsense layout done in classic style, with no shortage of photos to complement the text. The articles feature Southern beauty spots, historic houses, contemporary decoration, fairs, art, food, and culture.

Sports Illustrated. Time and Life Building, Rockefeller Center, New York 10020.

Great inspiration for displays on sports, whether it be fiction or nonfiction, can be obtained from this action-filled, colorfully laid-out magazine. It boasts superb action photos.

Stern. Gruner und Jahr Gmbh und Co., Warburgstrasse 50, 2000 Hamburg, West Germany.

In some ways like America's *Life* Magazine, *Stern* is a spicey, comprehensive look at European, particularly German, politics, food, sports, and gossip, with cleverly arranged layout and photos.

Time Out. Tower House, 374 Grays Inn Road, London WC1X 8BB.

This is the original weekly London entertainments guide, with feature articles and information about hundreds of weekly events: art, music, theater, cinema, jumble sales, children's events, gay happenings, and ballet. Its trendy layout reflects the London street scene. It is a great investment, even for out-of-towners, for its storehouse of ideas from the city that never sleeps.

Vogue. Vogue House, Hanover Square, London W1R OAD, or 350 Madison Avenue, New York 10017.

It could claim to be the world's classiest magazine. It is a storehouse of glamorous ideas for displays, both in photography and layout, with excellent ads.

(The World of) Interiors. 228 Fulham Road, London SW10.

This one could also claim to be the world's classiest magazine, since it offers a monthly glimpse into the exclusive lives and homes of the tasteful rich, mostly in Europe, often in America, with lavish displays of color photos classically arranged with text. The ads themselves can supply endless scope for display ideas; the small ads for specialist craftspersons and shops are especially notable.

INDEX